THE MACKINTOSH STYLE

ELIZABETH
WILHIDE

THE MACKINTOSH STYLE

DESIGN AND DECOR

CHRONICLE BOOKS
SAN FRANCISCO

First published in the United States by Chronicle Books.

Copyright © 1995 by Pavilion.
Text copyright © 1995 by Elizabeth Wilhide.
Printed in Italy.

Book design: David Fordham
Jacket design: Rebecca S. Neimark, Twenty-Six Letters

Library of Congress Cataloging-in-Publication Data:

Wilhide, Elizabeth.
The mackintosh style / by Elizabeth Wilhide.
160 p.   25.8 x 25.4 cm.
Includes bibliographical references and index.
ISBN 0-8118-1032-1
1. Mackintosh, Charles Rennie, 1868–1928—
Criticism and interpretation.
2. Arts and crafts movement—Scotland. I. Title.
N6797.M23W56   1995
709'.2—dc20   94-44478
CIP

Distributed in Canada by Raincoast Books
8680 Cambie Street
Vancouver, B.C., V6P 6M9

10 9 8 7 6 5 4 3 2 1

Chronicle Books
275 Fifth Street
San Francisco, CA 94103

CONTENTS

■ ■ ■

INTRODUCTION

CHARLES RENNIE MACKINTOSH IS SOMETHING OF AN ARCHITECTURAL ENIGMA. IN A TANTALIZINGLY short career he produced one undisputed masterpiece, the Glasgow School of Art, a small number of brilliantly realized public buildings, houses and interiors, as well as a wide range of innovative designs for furniture, textiles, wall decoration, artefacts and posters. At the end of his life he devoted his entire artistic attention to watercolour painting.

Mackintosh holds a special place in the history of design. The precise nature of his influence and the origins of his particular genius have nevertheless given rise to much debate among architectural critics and design historians. When Mackintosh's work was rescued from virtual oblivion in the mid-twentieth century, he was hailed as one of the most important precursors of the Modern movement; the Glasgow School of Art was acclaimed as the first truly modern building. In later appraisals this view was somewhat qualified and his work placed firmly in the context of Victorian progressive thought, a logical development of the ideals expressed by Pugin, Ruskin and Morris. More popularly, Mackintosh's name has become synonymous with the strange flowering of northern Art Nouveau, a style succinctly evoked by the attenuated verticals of his high-backed chairs or the graphic elegance of his letterforms.

Lone genius, prophetic architect, poet of the interior – there is much in Mackintosh's life and work to support a number of differing viewpoints. No one familiar with the development of contemporary

Charles Rennie Mackintosh (1868–1928), photographed in 1893 at the age of twenty-five by T. & R. Annan and Sons of Glasgow. One of a series of contemporary portraits of the dashing young 'artist-architect', this photograph shows a confident and determined Mackintosh in characteristically 'artistic' dress.

Mackintosh won many prizes and distinctions during his brilliant student career, including the prestigious Alexander Thomson Travelling Scholarship, which enabled him to spend several months touring Italy in 1891. The years of his greatest creative achievements were still to come.

design could fail to appreciate how the finest of Mackintosh's work at the Hill House and the School of Art uncannily anticipates the purity and structural integrity now identified with modernism. The white interiors, bold handling of materials and enlightened practicality seem to point firmly in the direction of the new design age.

To see Mackintosh solely as a visionary modernist, however, is misleading. Ornament was emphatically not a crime to Mackintosh; the decorative and expressive aspects of his work were integral. Inspired by nature and the traditions of his native country, his genius was to achieve a remarkable degree of synthesis between the decorative and the structural: it is his ability to resolve the tension between these two opposing elements which marks him as great.

Mackintosh was indeed a 'purifier in the field of architecture', in the words of Mies van der Rohe, but the poetic intensity of his work, where rationality is always clothed in an artistic sensibility, hints at deeper levels. Superficially, his work may appear pared down, but it is a simplicity which is infused with symbol and meaning. In this context, the creative partnership of Mackintosh and his wife, Margaret Macdonald, his devotion to nature and his desire to forge a new national style make better sense.

If genius, as Wilde said, is the infinite capacity for taking pains, Mackintosh was the embodiment of it. A fastidious and persistent attention to detail, a dogged refusal to compromise and a totality of vision which encompassed every fixture and fitting give his work a vigorous and distinctive unity. His buildings are inseparable from what they contain; every element, however minute, is considered in its relation to the whole. The result is a unique vocabulary of design and decoration.

The active and successful period of Mackintosh's working life occupies barely a decade, but it was a critical decade. Poised on the cusp of a new age, rooted in the old, Mackintosh's work is unlike, but not unconnected to, what had gone before; distinct, but not divorced, from the progression to a new architectural style. A designer of great originality and power, it was his personal misfortune that this proved not to be a triumphant stance, but an isolated one.

Sheer bad luck, professional setbacks and misunderstanding conspired to provide Mackintosh with what has been described as a 'tragically small range of opportunities'. A proud and difficult temperament only made matters worse and gave a sad inevitability to his decline. What began so brilliantly ended in self-imposed exile, near-penury and almost complete critical eclipse.

The poignancy of a life which failed to fulfil its dazzling promise is intensified by the great importance placed on Mackintosh's achievements today. In crude financial terms, a recent sale of Mackintosh drawings and furniture made the point very tellingly. An ironic postscript to the disappointment and hardship of his final years, the sale saw one of Mackintosh's high-backed chairs fetch over £300,000 ($465,000), the highest price ever paid for a twentieth-century chair, while an ebonized writing cabinet went for nearly £800,000 ($1,240,000). Yet at the time of the architect's death, a group of four chairs were valued at merely £1 ($1.55); the entire estate, which comprised the contents of two studios, was reckoned to be worth a pitiful £88 16s 2d ($136.40): 'practically of no value' in the words of the official assessors. Mackintosh buildings were still being demolished in Glasgow only twenty years ago.

Fritillaria **by Charles Rennie Mackintosh, 1915. This sensitive watercolour is one of many beautiful studies of flowers executed by Mackintosh during his sojourn in the small coastal village of Walberswick, Suffolk. The synthesis of his architectural and artistic vision is evident in the sinuous natural forms and the graphic chequered patterning.**

The obscurity which clouded the end of Mackintosh's life lasted long after his death. Sir Niklaus Pevsner was among the first to bring Mackintosh's work to critical attention in the 1930s; Dr Thomas Howarth did much to rehabilitate his reputation, writing the first and most definitive biography in 1952. In the course of Howarth's research, which began in 1940, he discovered a treasure trove of furniture, drawings and pictures stored in the basement of a Glasgow warehouse and was able to interview many of the architect's surviving friends and associates. These efforts at documentation, together with tireless campaigns to save what remained of Mackintosh's work from neglect and destruction, eventually fostered a growing awareness of his cultural importance. In 1968 a Centenary Exhibition was organized for the Edinburgh Festival Society; in 1982 the Hill House was acquired by the National Trust for Scotland; today, in Glasgow, plans are under way to construct Mackintosh's 'Art Lover's House', designed in 1901, as a postgraduate faculty of the School of Art. Some of Mackintosh's finest chair designs are in current production; the interiors of his former house on Southpark Avenue have been recreated in the Hunterian Art Gallery at Glasgow University. His name is now inextricably linked to the cultural identity of his native city.

Mackintosh's essentially incomplete and frustrated career tempt some to stake claims on his behalf, to read into his work intentions and aspirations that may or may not have been there. Ultimately it is more satisfying and constructive to focus on what Mackintosh did achieve, rather than what he might have done. A century later, we face many of the same dilemmas in design. How to give new life to old forms, how to reconcile tradition with change, how to express nature in building are questions which Mackintosh met head on and, for a short time, answered masterfully.

■ ■ ■

LIFE AND WORK

LIFE AND WORK

C HARLES RENNIE MACKINTOSH WAS BORN IN GLASGOW ON 7 JUNE 1868. HIS FATHER, WILLIAM MCINTOSH, was a superintendent of police, devout, upright and rather strict. His mother, Margaret Rennie, was a gentle woman, much loved by her family. In all there were to be eleven children, although it is thought that four or five did not survive childhood. Mackintosh was especially close to his eldest sister Isabella and his youngest sister Nancy.

EARLY YEARS

When Mackintosh was born, the family lived in a third-floor tenement flat in the east end of Glasgow. Ten years later his father had advanced sufficiently in his career to be able to move the growing family to Dennistoun, a quiet suburb on the outskirts of the city.

The little that is known of Mackintosh's early years provides few clues to the sources of his later artistic development. His school days were unremarkable, and neither parent seems to have shown any particular interest in the arts. William McIntosh, however, was a passionate gardener, devoting all his spare time to the pursuit. At Dennistoun he had access to a large plot in the grounds of a vacant property. 'The Garden of Eden', as it was nicknamed by the Mackintosh children, flourished under his care, and he encouraged his family to share his devotion to flowers.

Mackintosh was not a particularly robust child. One eyelid permanently drooped as a result of a childhood illness, and a slight muscular deformity in one foot – a contracted sinew – caused him to limp. Prescribed plenty of fresh air and exercise, he took to rambling over the Scottish countryside, sketching wild flowers and plants and making detailed drawings of local buildings. In these solitary

Mackintosh's last public commission was the design of Scotland Street School, Glasgow, completed in 1906. Working to an extremely restricted budget, and faced with considerable opposition, he created a forceful and dramatic composition dominated by twin glazed staircase towers serving as separate entrances for the sexes. The light, airy interior, human scale and attention to detail are characteristic of Mackintosh's best work. The building continued to function as a school until 1979. In 1990, it was renovated to Mackintosh's original designs and reopened as a Museum of Education.

excursions he learned a pattern of concentrated observation which remained with him for the rest of his life and forged an intense attachment to nature which informed all his work.

Mackintosh seems to have decided quite early on to become an architect and never deviated from this course, despite parental disapproval. In 1884, at the age of sixteen, having completed his schooling, he was apprenticed to the architectural firm of John Hutchison.

The following year, in a traumatic upheaval, Mackintosh's beloved mother died and his father remarried. The family subsequently moved several times, eventually settling in a terraced house on the south side of Glasgow, 27 Regent Park Square. Mackintosh appears to have remained living at home up until about the time of his marriage in 1900, converting a basement room into a workshop for his own use. In characteristic fashion, he adapted his surroundings to his increasingly particular taste, papering the walls in brown wrapping paper to which he added a stencilled frieze and removing an ornate fire surround to reveal a simple hob grate. Howarth notes that Mackintosh's sisters, willing assistants in his artistic endeavours despite their father's antipathy, believed the plain cottage style of the fireplace grate to have been the basis for Mackintosh's later designs.

■ ■ ■

APPREN-TICE SHIP & EDUC-ATION

IN THE CONTEXT OF MACKINTOSH'S EARLY DEVELOPMENT, IT IS IMPORTANT TO PROVIDE A PICTURE OF the city in which his talents were beginning to emerge. Glasgow, at the end of the nineteenth century, was no provincial backwater, but the 'second city of the Empire', a burgeoning industrial centre with a lively cultural life. Over half the world's sea-going ships were built and fitted out on the Clyde; the production of railway engines and carriages and textiles were other major industries. Occupying a strategic position between the markets of northern Europe and America, the city was renowned for its energy, technological advance and high educational standards.

Glasgow was not unconnected to the wider world of cultural development; some of those who had made their fortunes in the industrial and commercial expansion of the city became lively patrons of the arts. Towards the end of the century, local artists were also beginning to make their mark. A group of young painters in the impressionist manner, known collectively as the Glasgow Boys or Glasgow School, provoked much attention at home and abroad. The work of these men, Macaulay Stevenson, E. A. Walton, George Henry, James Guthrie, John Lavery and E. A. Hornel, among others, was exhibited in galleries and in other public and commercial buildings; the Glasgow Boys were later invited to exhibit with the Munich Secession in 1890. There were strong ties with groups of Continental artists, and with the Pre-Raphaelite movement in England, and an awareness of the work

Women students at work in the toplit Museum in the Glasgow School of Art, c. 1900. The school was noted for its progressive attitude to women's education.

of Aestheticists such as Whistler. Many of the Glaswegian artistic fraternity shared the contemporary fascination for Japanese art.

Glasgow's flourishing industries and associated trades had a voracious appetite for skilled craftsmen and technicians. It was to educate 'industrial artists' and 'ornamentalists' that the School of Art was founded in 1844. By the turn of the century, it has been estimated that nearly three thousand students were training in some form of design at Glasgow. Architectural training in Glasgow, as elsewhere in Britain in the late nineteenth century, was loosely organized on the basis of apprenticeship: architecture was as yet unrecognized as an academic discipline. For a nominal wage, or perhaps even a small fee, the apprentice absorbed what he could from a practising architect over a period of five years, the efficacy of the training depending to no small extent on the success of the office and scope of its work.

There was no formal requirement for any additional study, but the same year as his apprenticeship began, Mackintosh enrolled in evening classes at the Glasgow School of Art, where initially he took courses in painting and drawing. His formal architectural education began in his fourth year; he studied under Thomas Smith and the fine draughtsman Alexander McGibbon, who later became director of architectural studies at the School.

From the beginning Mackintosh distinguished himself as a student, winning many school prizes over the course of eight years' part-time attendance. More notably, Mackintosh's designs for a chapel

(1888) and a church (1889) won prizes when entered for the annual National Competition at South Kensington, to which many art schools submitted work. Both designs received favourable comments in the professional press.

Mackintosh arrived at the School of Art at a critical point in its history. The year after Mackintosh enrolled, a new head was appointed, a young Englishman named Francis Newbery. Newbery proved an able and inspiring Director, and with his awareness of progressive trends in art and design education (he had taught at South Kensington), he began to shift the emphasis of the School away from its practical origins in the direction of freer, more creative expression. By the 1890s the Glasgow School of Art had acquired the reputation as one of the finest institutions in Britain, and the student body had grown considerably.

Drawing was the foundation of the curriculum. In his inaugural address, Newbery stated:

All our great industries – whether of shipbuilding or house building, whether of engineering or machine-making, whether of pattern-making or the higher art of painting – must first have their origin in drawing, and without this basis none of them can be established. The shipbuilder must first design his model; the architect his structure; the engineer his railway, his docks or his bridges; the painter his sketch; and the designer his ideal, before he can begin his operations.

PROMINENT PROFILES.

"SCHOOL OF ART."

'Fra' Newbery, the energetic director of the School of Art, was the subject of this Prominent Profile *in the* Evening Times, **1903. He was described as possessing 'unusual powers as an organizer' in the accompanying biographical note.**

Newbery's stated aim was 'to practically supply that which Glasgow at present needs – namely a race of designers for her own creation'. He set up a committee of local architects to oversee architectural education at the School, introduced new craft classes and invited luminaries such as Walter Crane and William Morris to speak.

The institute which controlled art school teaching throughout Britain, the Department of Science and Art in South Kensington, promoted an analytic and 'scientific' approach to drawing. Under the 'National Course of Instruction', the curriculum which was compulsory until the 1880s, architectural students learned perspective and technical drawing, copied various forms of ornament and studied the components of classical styles. As the rules relaxed and the curriculum finally ceased to be compulsory in 1901, Newbery was able to introduce a new approach, based on Ruskin's idea of drawing as the direct observation of nature, a representation of apparent reality rather than a dissected analysis of structure.

Mackintosh's practical apprenticeship, which taught him the fundamentals of building technique, was therefore supplemented by an art school curriculum which introduced him to the full vocabulary of historical ornament, while offering significant scope for a more creative and individual expression.

Mackintosh believed that true architecture must embrace all the arts, whether fine or applied, that 'there must be a real communion and a working together'. His holistic approach owed much to the nature of his education.

In 1889, at the age of twenty-one, Mackintosh completed his articles and secured the position of junior draughtsman with Honeyman and Keppie, a large and successful Glasgow practice. The following year, he won the prestigious Alexander Thomson Travelling Scholarship for his original design for 'a public hall in the early classical style'. The award – the then princely sum of £60 ($93) – enabled Mackintosh in 1891 to take a leave of absence from Honeyman and Keppie and spend several months travelling abroad.

It was, in a sense, the true culmination of his architectural education and the beginning of his independent career. Mackintosh's Grand Tour was pursued with energy and enthusiasm and, like generations of Grand Tourists before him, he focused his attention on the museums, monuments and great public buildings of Italy. His diary, which survives, diligently records his impressions of all that he saw, illuminated with flashes of insight, intensity of emotion and wry amusement. Equally valuably, he passed much time sketching details, executing fine drawings in pencil and wash, and making watercolours, often combining several media. His attention fell as much on the features and furnishings of buildings as their general architectural or structural character. A selection of drawings which he sent home from Italy for entry into the School of Art Student's Club annual exhibition won first prize.

In February 1891, just before his departure for Italy, Mackintosh was invited to read a paper to the Glasgow Architectural Association. His chosen subject was Scotch Baronial architecture. This address represents the first expression of the ideas and beliefs which were to underlie all his architectural work. Here Mackintosh presented a forceful and impassioned plea for a 'native' style in the Scottish Baronial tradition:

It was . . . the architecture of our own country, just as much Scotch as we are ourselves – as indigenous to our country as our wild flowers, our family names, our customs or our political constitution.

He accepted that many features of this tradition had been absorbed from other cultures, specifically from France, but he laid particular importance on the way elements had been adapted to suit the Scottish climate and local materials. He praised 'genuineness and utility' in architecture; and buildings whose form sprang from layout and plan rather than those whose style was artificially imposed. He also warned that traditional forms should not be copied wholesale without paying attention to modern needs.

It was a truly personal statement; in describing how some would venture down 'muddy roads and snowy path, and with glowing heart but shivering hand . . . sketch . . . the venerable castle with feelings of the most indescribable delight' he was, of course, referring to his own favourite pursuit since boyhood. Mackintosh was only twenty-three when he addressed his audience, which must have included members of the Glaswegian architectural establishment, successful exponents of the architectural style he was implicitly criticizing, namely the Greek Revival. The lecture, and the prize-winning Italian drawings, crucially brought him to the attention of Francis Newbery, who was to be his most important and influential ally.

Up to this point, Mackintosh's architectural designs and competition entries provide little evidence of his future direction; and neither, to a large extent, do the two schemes he entered for the Soane Medallion competition in 1892 and 1893, the first of which was a chapter house in the classical manner, the second a Gothic-style railway terminus. This is unsurprising, since success in competitions and the consequent publicity was the chief means of getting established in the profession in the days before architectural diploma courses, and official recognition generally depended on achieving a degree of academic excellence within prescribed limits, rather than breaking new ground. It was not to be long, however, before Mackintosh showed signs of independence.

Mackintosh photographed in 1898 with the young Hamish Davidson at the family home 'Gladsmuir', Kilmacolm.

■ ■ ■

THE FOUR

THE TRUE FLAVOUR OF A DECADE IS SUPPOSED ONLY TO EMERGE A FEW YEARS AFTER ITS CHRONOLOGICAL beginning; if that is true, 1893, which saw the first publication of *The Studio*, marks the start of the nineties, with its peculiar mixture of *fin-de-siècle* decadence and progressive thought.

Many of those who have written about Mackintosh, as well as contemporaries such as Jessie Newbery, the wife of Francis Newbery, have stressed the importance of *The Studio* in the development of the Mackintosh style. The first issues of the influential magazine included Beardsley's illustrations for Oscar Wilde's *Salome*, Jan Toorop's mystical painting *The Three Brides* and the designs and views of C. F. A. Voysey, then emerging as a leading exponent of a radically simplified vernacular tradition. In the first issue Voysey wrote:

To go to Nature is, of course, to approach the fountainhead, but a literal transcript will not result in good ornament; before a living plant a man must go through an elaborate process of selection and analysis . . . if he does this, although he has gone directly to Nature, his work will not resemble any of his predecessors; he has become an inventor . . . we are at once relieved from restrictions of style and period, and can live and work in the present . . .

To Mackintosh, searching for a way of translating the inspiration of nature and the native traditions of his own country into a new style, these words must have struck a powerful chord. At Honeyman and Keppie he had met and formed a friendship with Herbert MacNair, a draughtsman in the same office, who was also enrolled at the Glasgow School of Art. The two men found they shared an enthusiasm for sketching the Scottish countryside, and an interest in graphic experiment. From a modern standpoint, an interest in letterforms and graphic representation may appear to have little relevance to the fundamental problems of creating a new architectural style. For Mackintosh and his contemporaries, however, drawing was the means not only of expressing ideas but the primary vehicle of discovery and invention.

Cabbages in an Orchard, 1894. This watercolour by Mackintosh, published in a magazine produced by students at the School of Art, has been interpreted by some critics, notably Timothy Neat, as Mackintosh's allegory of the sterility and corruption of contemporary architectural practice. The imagery of decay, ugliness and lack of vitality conveyed by the cabbages in their forlorn setting summarized Mackintosh's belief that architecture had lost touch with its living roots.

Around this time, Francis Newbery noticed that the work of Mackintosh and MacNair displayed a striking similarity to that of two other students at the School, Frances and Margaret Macdonald, and promptly introduced them to each other. 'The Four', as they were quickly named, formed a close collaboration founded on artistic sympathy. MacNair may already have been working along similar lines when he met Mackintosh, and there is too little information about the Macdonald sisters' early lives to trace their artistic development, but what is clear is that The Four quickly evolved their own distinctive style, and one which attracted immediate attention.

From around 1893 onwards. The Four experimented in different media, expressing their ideas in beaten metalwork, stained glass, embroidery and gesso as well as drawing and illustration. The characteristics of their style – stylized natural forms, strong vertical emphasis, flowing curves held in check by rigorous geometric organization – translated readily into different materials and diverse

The Tree of Personal Effort, 1895. **This painting depicts three abstract tree forms flourishing in the light of the sun, representing creativity and artistic growth. As Mackintosh said in his 1893 lecture, 'And still you ask what is the connection between Architecture and Painting! Everything.'**

objects. Posters designed by Mackintosh between 1895 and 1896 provoked great interest and some adverse comment. In 1897 the editor of *The Studio* agreed that Mackintosh's posters may be 'somewhat trying to the average person' in their 'perversion of humanity' but defended them on the basis that when 'a man has something to say and knows how to say it the conversion of others is usually but a question of time'.

During this same period Mackintosh began to design furniture, and in 1895 rented a studio where he could carry out various commissions away from home. He produced a number of pieces for a Glasgow firm of cabinet-makers, Guthrie and Wells, mainly simple cabinets and wardrobes with minimal decoration and plain, natural or stained finishes.

After graduation from the School, the Macdonald sisters had opened their own studio, where they sold their work; in 1895 MacNair left Honeyman and Keppie and also set up on his own to concentrate on furniture design and craftwork. The studios of The Four became something of a focus for young artists and those involved with Glasgow's cultural life, and there were many parties and late night discussions. Keppie, the junior partner at Honeyman and Keppie, often invited Mackintosh and MacNair to his home at Ayr for the weekend, where the gathering might include the Macdonalds and other women artists. The guests were put up in two rented bungalows nearby known as 'The Roaring Camp'.

Mackintosh was a particularly lively and gregarious member of an enthusiastic and sociable group. A photograph taken in 1893, when he was twenty-five, shows a confident and handsome individual, with dark Highland colouring and wearing 'artistic' dress. Popular, energetic, kind and generous, he loved to talk, and his glittering student reputation was beginning to spread to a wider audience. The other side of his complex personality was also evident. He could be stubborn to the point of arrogance, proud and remote; in boyhood he had been prone to quite violent outbursts of rage which went beyond the usual childhood tantrums. Howarth notes tactfully that he was never particularly 'temperate' even as a student, but at this stage in his career the stresses placed on his personality by his vast creative energies and devotion to detail had not yet begun to take their toll.

Outside Glasgow, the work of The Four also began to attract notice. In 1896 they were invited to exhibit at the influential Arts and Crafts Society Exhibition in London, an important event then held every three years. Asked for work in the 'modern style', they sent posters on which MacNair collaborated, a watercolour by Mackintosh, a pair of beaten metal panels and a silver clock case by the Macdonald sisters and a hall settle by Mackintosh.

The work was widely met with protest and dismay, and much scorn was heaped on the distorted human figures that were a characteristic feature of the style. For these so-called perversions, and the mood of mysticism and melancholy which permeated the paintings of the Macdonald sisters in particular, The Four were unkindly labelled 'The Spook School'. As a group they were never invited to exhibit in England again, although Mackintosh sent some of his own work to later Arts and Crafts exhibitions in 1899, 1916 and 1923.

Some critics have identified this unfortunate episode as a lost opportunity of tragic proportions. The rejection of Mackintosh at a critical stage in his career by the Arts and Crafts practitioners, many of whose views he shared, effectively cut him off from future advancement. Others believe that

'The Immortals', the self-styled group of young artists who gathered for holiday weekends at Keppie's home, c. 1893. In the foreground are Herbert MacNair and Charles Rennie Mackintosh; seated behind at the far left is Margaret Macdonald; at the right of the group are Jessie Keppie (then Mackintosh's fiancée) and her brother John Keppie. The figure at the rear is Frances Macdonald.

Mackintosh, while undoubtedly disappointed by his reception, recognized the significant ways in which his work was beginning to diverge from Arts and Crafts ideals.

Some good, however, did come of the Arts and Crafts débâcle. Gleeson White, the editor of *The Studio*, was intrigued by the young designers and went to visit them on home ground. His favourable impressions, published in the magazine, complete with illustrations of their work, eventually came to the attention of Alexander Koch in Darmstadt, publisher of the progressive magazine *Dekorative Kunst*, and Mackintosh's important ties to the new Continental art movement were forged.

For three of The Four, the new style was an end in itself and they progressed little beyond it; for Mackintosh alone it was a point of departure. The decorative invention of this experimental period and the insights he gained were to feed his architectural imagination in years to come and take on their own distinctive path of development.

The Four ceased to collaborate directly in 1898, when MacNair accepted the post of Instructor in Decorative Design at Liverpool University. The following year, he married Frances, the younger of the two English-born Macdonald sisters, and they settled on Merseyside. In August 1900, Mackintosh and Margaret Macdonald, who had continued to work closely together in Glasgow, were married in a quiet ceremony.

Mackintosh was thirty-two at the time of his marriage; his wife was three years older. Margaret was a tall and stately woman with abundant coppery hair; photographs show her wearing the 'reformed' dress favoured by the artistic and progressive. Over the years much controversy has surrounded her role in the evolution of the Mackintosh style. Those who champion Mackintosh as a prophet of modernism find the more mystical and decorative nature of Margaret's work an embarrassment; some have even implied that her apparent lack of 'progress' from the style of The Four was somehow detrimental to the full development of Mackintosh as a designer. Others find much evidence of a shared imagination, a true marriage of minds. In one recent essay, Margaret Macdonald is described as the 'spiritual key to Mackintosh's greatness'; justification for this view can be seen in Mackintosh's constant striving to reconcile what are traditionally seen as the 'masculine' qualities of structure and form with the more 'feminine' role of decoration. There is no suggestion in any of his work that he was prepared to jettison one aspect in favour of the other.

It is clear that Mackintosh himself found Margaret's contribution invaluable. In his own estimation, his wife had genius, he had only talent. Margaret created decorations and artefacts for many of her husband's interiors, and the homes they made together bear witness to a deep

Margaret Macdonald Mackintosh, photographed c. 1905. She is seated in front of a white painted desk designed by Mackintosh in 1900. The desk is enriched with silvered copper panels probably worked by Margaret herself. The coloured glass inserts that decorated the piece originally are now missing. To Mackintosh, Margaret was more than a muse; their life together was one of shared artistic and spiritual outlook.

artistic compatibility, a unified endeavour. Mackintosh often signed his paintings with his wife's initials as well as his own, and it must be assumed that this was not merely a chivalrous gesture, but an acknowledgement of the indivisibility of their outlook. They were, as one friend later recalled, 'hand in glove throughout their lives'. The marriage, although childless, was to prove more than resilient in misfortune, and provided Mackintosh with much-needed stability and support. In this lifelong creative partnership, the spirit of The Four was kept alive.

■ ■ ■

EARLY PRO-FESSIONAL LIFE

'WE MUST CLOTHE MODERN IDEAS WITH MODERN DRESS – ADORN OUR DESIGNS WITH LIVING FANCY.' Addressing the Glasgow Institute of Architects in 1893, Mackintosh ventured considerably further down the path he had first taken with his paper on Scottish Baronial architecture two years previously. 'Old architecture lived because it had a purpose. Modern architecture, to be real, must not be a mere envelope without contents.' In provocative and passionate terms, he argued the case for modernity in design, decrying the type of historical fakery which resulted in 'modern churches, theatres, banks, museums, exchanges, Municipal Buildings, Art Galleries, etc., etc., made in imitations of Greek temples'.

As many have pointed out, Mackintosh borrowed almost the entire text of his paper directly from W. R. Lethaby's book, *Architecture, Mysticism and Myth*. While the words may not have been his own – and many of his public pronouncements owed debts to some previously published text or other – what counted was the undoubted sincerity of his belief. Mackintosh was coming to the point where he would soon be able to put these ideas into practice.

From the early period of Mackintosh's employment at Honeyman and Keppie, three buildings in particular show evidence of his involvement in their design; perspective drawings by Mackintosh of all three buildings survive. In the Glasgow Herald Building (designed 1893–4) it is the form of the corner tower, and the proportions and positioning of windows along one façade which hint at his input.

Queen Margaret's Medical College (designed 1894), a women's medical school, is more revealing. Here a central two-storey hall is the focus for an informal layout of internal spaces, the staircase tower has tall narrow windows positioned to conform with the ascent of the stairs, and the steeply pitched roof is a traditionally Scottish feature which recurs again and again in Mackintosh's later work. The client for the building, Professor Thomas H. Bryce, later recalled Mackintosh as a young apprentice working on the design with Keppie, with special responsibility for the decoration. On one occasion, Mackintosh asked to look down Bryce's microscope. What he saw – a developing fish eye – so entranced him that he immediately made a drawing of it, later admitting that it had formed the basis for many fruitful decorative ideas. What is interesting about this story, aside from the vivid glimpse it provides of an artist at work, is the indication of how Mackintosh was beginning to forge a powerful creative link between his graphic experiments with The Four and his architectural ideas.

The third building in this transitional period was the Martyr's Public Schol (designed 1895). In this building, Mackintosh began to show the striking unity of structure and decoration which was fundamental to his work. In the exposed timber roof of the hall, the king posts form stylized tulip shapes; in the stairwell pairs of vertical trusses are emphasized with inverted heart cut-outs where they meet the horizontal joists. As one critic, David Brett, has pointed out, Mackintosh's 'principal intention is not to express the structure, but to give us the experience of structuring', a subtle but critical difference and one which lends his work a dynamic intensity. Exposed joints and structural members were common enough in the work of progressive contemporary designers; in Mackintosh's case, such 'honesty' did not always tally with the structural realities but was employed to evoke powerful images of assembly.

■ ■ ■

GLAS-
:G⁰W
1896-1914

THE CHRONOLOGY OF ANY ARCHITECTURAL CAREER IS COMPLICATED BY THE FACT THAT BUILDINGS ARE exceptionally slow to realize. In Mackintosh's case, the time of his greatest productivity, which saw the completion of the masterpieces on which his fame rests, occupies little more than a decade; after 1906 he was already beginning to lapse into obscurity. This intense period begins with the competition for the design of the Glasgow School of Art, and ends with the completion of its final phase.

For Mackintosh, more than other architects, design was a continuous process, which did not cease once a building was on site; this evolving development brings added complexities to the story. To avoid unnecessary fragmentation, Mackintosh's principal architectural, interior and design projects will be examined in closer detail in subsequent chapters and mentioned briefly here in the context of his personal history.

1896 was a turning-point for Mackintosh. In that year, the year of the Arts and Crafts Society Exhibition, he conceived the initial design of the Glasgow School of Art and met Miss Cranston, who would be an important patron of his work for the next twenty years.

On the face of it, the Glasgow School of Art, Mackintosh's finest architectural achievement, appears to have sprung from nowhere, a radical and fully conceived modern building created by a young architect of conventional training in a provincial city. The facts tell a different story. The School of Art, Mackintosh's first true commission, was also in a sense his last major work, the final stages of the building being completed in 1909. In the intervening period Mackintosh's architectural vision developed considerably, and the final building is as much a product of this process as it is of its initial conception. Viewed in the context of Mackintosh's experiments with The Four, and his search for a new graphic language, the design for the School is a natural progression, a translation of ideas first explored in other media into built form.

Immediately after Mackintosh completed his initial drawings for the School, he designed Queen's Cross Church (built in 1897–9); since 1977 the building has served as the headquarters of the Charles Rennie Mackintosh Society. The church, with its exposed steel roof ties, is a modern reinterpretation of traditional forms; in the detailing more characteristic features emerge. The pulpit is carved with stylized tulips; the form of the stained-glass windows and the gallery balustrades, with their pierced pendant posts, prefigure later work.

Another Honeyman and Keppie project from this period was the Daily Record Building in Renfield Lane (designed 1900–1901), now owned by an insurance company. Mackintosh skilfully counteracted a dark, narrow, enclosed site by cladding the four storeys above ground level in white glazed brick. The vigorous design of the façade features a version of Mackintosh's 'tree of life' motif executed in a pattern of projecting bricks.

In 1899, Mackintosh received his first significant commission independent of Honeyman and Keppie, to build a family house for William Davidson, a local businessman and art collector. Here, at Windyhill, and at The Hill House, built for the Blackie family between 1902 and 1904, he created his own version of Scottish vernacular, radically simplified and updated for modern living. The Hill House, in particular, where Mackintosh had full control of the design down to the last detail, displays the true character of his approach unhampered by the constraints of an existing building.

Mackintosh's early involvement with Miss Cranston, the eccentric, energetic proprietor of successful Glasgow tea rooms, was initially limited to a collaborative role with the designer George Walton, Mackintosh contributing mural decorations under Walton's direction at the Buchanan Street premises and furniture for the Argyle Street Tea Rooms in 1897. After 1900, Mackintosh was in sole charge of Miss Cranston's projects, completely designing the interiors and their contents at Ingram Street and, finally, creating both interiors and exterior at the Willow Tea Rooms in Sauchiehall Street (1903–1904), his most accomplished and progressive work in that context.

Between 1904 and 1909 Mackintosh also carried out alterations and decorations to Hous'hill, near Glasgow (demolished 1933), the home of Miss Cranston and her husband Major Cochrane. Most significant was his design for the music room, which

Daily Record Buildings, Renfield Lane, Glasgow. This 1901 perspective, executed in watercolour, and taken from the southeast, reveals Mackintosh's response to the restrictions of the site. The upper storeys of the building are clad in white glazed brick and the facade is decorated with three stylized trees.

DAILY RECORD BUILDINGS

Mackintosh's perspective drawing of The Hill House, 1903. The Hill House, designed for Walter Blackie, is the finest of all Mackintosh's domestic buildings. It is now owned by the National Trust for Scotland and is open to the public.

featured an open timber screen echoing the form of a curved end wall. At Hous'hill, too, he was able to design a far wider range of furniture than for either of his previous domestic commissions; although the Hous'hill interiors were destroyed by fire, some of these exquisite pieces survive.

Many of the characteristic features of Mackintosh's interiors first appeared in the context of his own home, which he and Margaret decorated and furnished just before their wedding in 1900. The flat at 120 Mains Street, where they lived until 1906, was astonishingly sparse and simple for its day. Its power derived from an embracing unity of design: everything down to the cutlery was designed or made by the Mackintoshes. Walls were largely white or light-coloured, except for the dining-room which was dark; floors were covered in grey carpet and much of the furniture was enamelled white. When the Mackintoshes eventually moved to 6 Florentine Terrace (later 78 Southpark Avenue), they took many of the fittings and pieces of furniture with them to be installed in their new house.

In later years Mary Newbery Sturrock, the daughter of Francis Newbery, recalled the serenity of those rooms, where every aspect had received the same care and attention, down to the two grey cushions placed either side of the fireplace for the Mackintoshes' two grey Persian cats. In these elegant, scrupulously arranged surroundings, the Mackintoshes hosted tea parties long remembered for their exquisite refinement and discussed the latest artistic and intellectual developments with their friends. Mackintosh, at this most intensely creative period, exuded an air of brooding energy, which led one visitor to the Mains Street flat to compare him to an evangelical American clergyman. His nickname 'Tosh' or 'Toshie' ('Uncle Tosh' to younger friends) suggests the gentler side of his personality.

In 1901, on the retirement of John Honeyman, Mackintosh became a senior partner in the firm, which was now known as Honeyman, Keppie and Mackintosh. In the same year he began work on the design of the Scotland Street School. The building is distinguished by a simple plan, symmetrically arranged to segregate the sexes, and twin three-storey staircase bays infilled with windows. Decoration is minimal, a reflection both of a restricted budget and the functional nature of the building, and this sense of restraint underlines the modernity of the approach. The following year saw Mackintosh embark on the revisions for the final phase of the Art School, a stage which included what is regarded as the finest of all his designs, the Library.

From the turn of the century onwards, Mackintosh's work has met with increasing interest on the Continent. In 1898 Alexander Koch published an article about the Glasgow designers in *Dekorative Kunst*; in 1900 both the Mackintoshes and the MacNairs were invited to Vienna to participate in the 8th Secessionist Exhibition. Their contribution, a furnished and decorated room, made use of elements already created for clients at home and received much critical acclaim. Other European

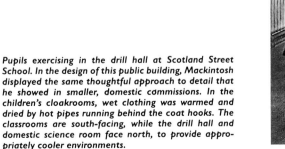

Pupils exercising in the drill hall at Scotland Street School. In the design of this public building, Mackintosh displayed the same thoughtful approach to detail that he showed in smaller, domestic commissions. In the children's cloakrooms, wet clothing was warmed and dried by hot pipes running behind the coat hooks. The classrooms are south-facing, while the drill hall and domestic science room face north, to provide appropriately cooler environments.

exhibitions followed, notably at Turin in 1902, through which valuable contact with progressive designers in Austria was established and maintained; Mackintosh was much encouraged by the enthusiastic, near adulatory reception for his work in Europe. In 1902 Windyhill and other projects were published in *Dekorative Kunst*; in 1905 The Hill House was featured in *Deutsche Kunst und Dekoration*. Attention, however, was focused on Mackintosh's furniture and interior designs rather than his architectural achievements, and, except for three minor decorative commissions, one of which was the much admired music salon for Fritz Wärndorfer in Vienna (1902), little work came his way through this connection.

At home, despite continuing exposure in *The Studio* and the architectural critic Hermann Muthesius's attempts to champion his efforts, Mackintosh remained largely unregarded. *The Studio* published photographs of interiors from the first stage of the School of Art in 1900, the Mains Street flat in 1901, and the Argyle Street Tea Rooms in 1906. Muthesius featured the Mains Street flat in his influential book *Das englische Haus* (1904); his support and friendship were much valued and may have been influential in getting Mackintosh recognized among Continental designers. In England, however, Mackintosh was unable to shake off the Spook School label.

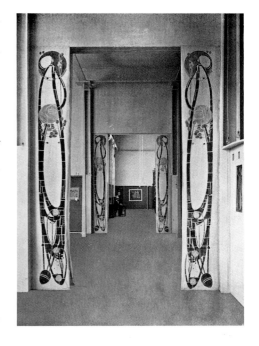

Banner-like stencilled panels framing the entrance to the three bays of the Scottish section at the International Exhibition of Modern Decorative Art, Turin, 1902. Newbery chose Mackintosh to design the room settings and display areas. The banners were created on site.

Three unsuccessful competition designs indicate what Mackintosh might have achieved given the opportunity. The first, in 1898, was a design for buildings to house the International Exhibition to be held in Glasgow in 1901. Mackintosh's submission, one of three made by Honeyman and Keppie, was radical and almost playful in conception. The second, and more important, was an entry for an international competition sponsored by the *Zeitschrift für Innendekoration* in 1901. The brief was to design a house for an 'art-lover': *Das Haus eines Kunstfreundes*. Mackintosh's scheme was a masterful expression of his unique graphic language, expressed in a clear and logical plan and robust structural form. No winner was declared, and the first prize was shared among sixteen entrants; Baillie Scott, often credited as the winner, was awarded second place. Mackintosh, who broke the rules by submitting an incorrect number of interior perspectives, was awarded a special prize. The third major competition (1902) was for the design of Liverpool Cathedral. His submission, a modern interpretation of the Gothic, betrays his deep interest in reworking and revitalizing traditional forms.

The tortuous chronology of these few years provides some indication of the pressures of Mackintosh's creative life. During this time, it must be remembered, he was engaged in the design not only of buildings, but of much of what they contained, from furniture to light fittings, cutlery to cupboards. The first stage of the design of the Glasgow Art School he described as 'a daily fight over

IDEENWETTBEWERB FÜR EIN HERRSCHAFTLICHES WOHNHAUS EINES KUNST-FREUNDES 14:

DAS SPEISE -=- ZIMMER:

C. R. MACKINTOSH. GLASGOW. HAUS EINES KUNST-FREUNDES.
VERLAGS-ANSTALT: ALEXANDER KOCH-DARMSTADT. - TAFEL XIV

Perspective of the dining room, Haus eines Kunstfreundes, 1901. Mackintosh's scheme for an 'Art-lover's House', never realized in his lifetime, is currently being built to the original design. The house, situated in Glasgow's Bellahouston Park, will eventually function as an international study centre.

three years', and undoubtedly it had drained his resources. By the second stage, which proceeded no less contentiously, his contact with the Secessionists, Olbrich, Hoffman, Moser and others, who were making rapid advances in Europe, had given him a stark comparison with his own lack of recognition and progress.

Following the establishment of the Wiener Werkstätte in 1903, Mackintosh was invited to set up a studio and metal workshop in Vienna, an offer which he declined. His status in Europe as a leading designer in the new art movement encouraged him for a time to believe a similar artistic revival could be brought about in his native country, whose landscape, flora and vernacular traditions had informed his entire architectural and graphic imagination. It was in Scotland that Mackintosh most wanted to succeed. 'It is indeed a great delight to oppose an all powerful enemy, and this is precisely the reason why Charles Rennie Mackintosh is working in Glasgow,' acknowledged an article in *Dekorative Kunst* in 1906. Quite how powerful and entrenched were the opponents of the new style Mackintosh had yet to discover.

After 1910, work began to tail away. There were a few domestic commissions – Mosside at Kilmacolm and Auchenibert at Killearn the most notable – but none fulfilled the promise shown so demonstrably by the designer of The Hill House. Aside from two further tea-room interiors for Miss Cranston, Mackintosh produced very little between 1910 and 1913.

The struggle to win recognition and creative scope for his architectural powers exhausted and embittered him. In Glasgow, the tea rooms were popularly considered to be something of a joke, and the School of Art was widely regarded as an oddity. The plans for the Scotland Street School were only approved after endless disputes. Faced with implacable indifference from his peers and outright hostility from official authorities, Mackintosh became

The drawing room fireplace at The Hill House, 1903, has a mosaic surround with five drop-shaped panels of mirrored and coloured glass inlay, creating a shimmering focus of interest for the 'winter end' of the room. A pair of steel straps suspend the fire-irons. The entire design has an arresting modernity.

depressed and increasingly turned to drink. Another architect was engaged to complete Auchenibert; Mackintosh is said to have spent most of the afternoons when he was supposed to have been on site at the public house in the village. At Honeyman and Keppie, his autocratic manner, muddled routines and erratic hours put the office under an intolerable strain, although some of the more extreme stories put about by colleagues after his departure must be discounted as sheer malicious exaggeration.

A perfectionist to the nth degree, Mackintosh's method of working was nevertheless calculated to cause friction. He typically redrafted designs over and over and did not hesitate to effect major changes while a building was in progress, an approach which naturally cost a great deal of time, money and goodwill. His remarkable attention to the intricacies of detail, insistence on the highest levels of workmanship and fierce intolerance of those who did not share his views won him few friends. As his isolation deepened, he became increasingly intractable and hypersensitive to criticism. To some, these intense periods of creative activity, the obsessive perfectionism, furious outbursts and melancholia suggest the manic-depressive temperament not uncommon in artists of genius.

To whatever degree the stresses were self-imposed, his work was bound to suffer. Clients began to complain, and in 1913 the inevitable happened with Mackintosh's resignation from Honeyman, Keppie and Mackintosh, a dispute over a competition entry nominally forcing the issue. Mackintosh's relationship with Keppie had long been difficult; an early estrangement was supposedly caused when Mackintosh jilted Keppie's sister Jessie to marry Margaret. Keppie tolerated but never actively supported his brilliant partner, and it is clear that Mackintosh viewed him as one of those establishment figures who effectively barred his progress.

■ ■ ■

FINAL YEARS

AFTER A SHORT-LIVED ATTEMPT TO PRACTISE ON HIS OWN, MORE OR LESS doomed from the start, Mackintosh turned his back on his native city in utter despondency. In 1914, shutting up their home on Southpark Avenue, the Mackintoshes departed for the coastal village of Walberswick in Suffolk.

The Newberys owned a holiday cottage at Walberswick; the village was popular with artists, particularly during the summer months. Margaret hoped that the peaceful surroundings would restore her husband's health and equilibrium, and they took a small riverside studio where they could work. Mackintosh immersed himself in painting, producing some of his finest studies of flowers, gathering material which he hoped to publish in Germany. During their time in Suffolk, war was declared. The Mackintoshes stayed on after the summer visitors had departed and began to attract suspicion. Mackintosh's habit of walking about the countryside at night, his deerstalker hat and Inverness cape, and even his Scots accent – exotic and alien in rural Suffolk – marked him as a foreign spy in the eyes of the locals. One evening when the Mackintoshes were out walking, soldiers raided their lodgings and found correspondence from Vienna, including an invitation from Secessionist architects to visit them. Mackintosh was summoned before magistrates and only managed to clear his name with some difficulty.

Mackintosh, a patriot, was outraged at the ignominy of it all. This bizarre and farcical episode, however, was the least of his misfortunes. The war effectively severed his ties with his greatest supporters in Europe, and after it was over the world had changed irrevocably and a new generation of designers were coming to the fore.

After Walberswick, the Mackintoshes took refuge in London, settling in Chelsea in 1915. They found friends among artists there and rented a couple

Margaret Macdonald Mackintosh, photographed by T. & R. Annan and Sons, Glasgow c. 1900, around the time of her marriage to Mackintosh. She is seated in the oak lug chair Mackintosh designed for the fireside of the drawing room at 120 Mains Street, Glasgow.

of adjacent studios in Glebe Place. Although the war had brought building work to a virtual halt, Mackintosh managed to secure a small commission the following year. The client, W. J. Bassett-Lowke, who owned a model-making firm, asked Mackintosh to carry out alterations to a small Victorian terraced house in Northampton, No. 78 Derngate. He had planned to build a new house but was unable to do so, owing to wartime restrictions.

In the strikingly original Derngate interiors and the small rear extension to the house Mackintosh appears to have anticipated decorative and architectural trends to come. Overall the scheme teemed with new ideas, and indicates that far from abandoning his architectural aspirations, Mackintosh was still evolving and changing his approach. The inspiration behind Derngate owed much to his association with the Austrian designers but was not derivative in any sense of Continental work.

For the next few years, the Mackintoshes made their living designing fabrics, selling watercolours and engaging in small decorative projects, some of which were commissioned by colleagues of Bassett-Lowke. They became involved with a dramatic group, designing sets and costumes, and played an active part in the social life of the Chelsea community. Throughout they maintained contact with old friends; Francis Newbery had retired and moved to Corfe Castle, and the Mackintoshes were frequent winter guests at the Newberys' house in there.

Le Fort Maillert, **1927. The watercolours Mackintosh painted during his final years in France, after renouncing architecture for good, are powerful studies of landscape and buildings. These late works impressed Salvador Dali so much that he claimed Mackintosh was 'a much greater artist than Cezanne'.**

During 1920 Mackintosh was engaged on a number of projects which had come his way through his involvement with the Chelsea circle of artists. He was commissioned to design a number of studios; the one scheme which proceeded was for the artist Harold Squire. The finished building apparently pleased the client but was only occupied for two years. A more ambitious venture was the proposal to create two blocks of studios for the Arts League of Service, an idealistic enterprise whose aim was to encourage the arts in general and, in this instance, to provide struggling artists with accommodation. The site for the scheme was next to Squire's studio. Mackintosh's designs were not well received by the LCC authorities, who found them too brutally utilitarian, and although permission was eventually granted, work never proceeded. A similar fate befell Mackintosh's design for a theatre for Margaret Morris, who ran a dance school in Chelsea. This design, formal, symmetrical and somewhat Secessionist in feeling, aroused even greater hostility. It is probable that lack of funds played a part in the failure of these schemes; Mackintosh's designs, as ever, showed little acknowledgement of financial constraints.

After 1920 work dwindled still further. The publisher Walter Blackie, who had been the client of Mackintosh's finest domestic building, The Hill House, helped out with a commission to design covers

Port Vendres, c. 1926. Port Vendres, a small Mediterranean port near the Franco-Spanish border, was the winter home of the Mackintoshes during their four-year stay in France. The robust drawing and luminous washes of pure colour display Mackintosh's mastery of the watercolour medium.

for booklets. The Mackintoshes carried on with their textile designs for Templetons in Glasgow, Liberty and Foxton's in London and Sefton's in Belfast, and continued to paint, but it was clear that there was to be no revival of Mackintosh's architectural career. He lapsed again into depression. Advised by their friend, the Scottish painter J. D. Ferguson, who was married to Margaret Morris, the Mackintoshes decided to take a long holiday abroad. They departed for the south of France in 1923; they were to remain there for four years.

The Mackintoshes stayed in a number of Pyrenean and Mediterranean villages, including Collioure, a small fishing village frequented by French artists. Later they installed themselves in the Hôtel de Commerce, Port Vendres, a larger port near the Spanish border. They found the climate congenial, the local people and food to their liking, and the cost of living agreeably low. For these remaining

Mackintosh photographed by E. O. Hoppé c. 1920. In stark comparison to the confident young architect of the 1893 Annan portrait, this image reveals the brooding melancholy and disillusionment of the later years. The Mackintoshes left Glasgow for good in 1914.

years, Mackintosh finally renounced all architectural ambitions, and turned his attention to watercolour painting, perfecting his technique with the same obsessive care he devoted to any creative enterprise. He produced both botanical studies of flowers and plants and powerful, architectonic studies of local scenes, such as *The Fort Maillert* and *The Rocks*, both of 1927. As with his flower studies, which seem to distil the essence of natural life, these late landscapes are imbued with his architectural vision. As Robert Macleod has written: 'In a curious and poignant sense these paintings could have been built.'

In 1927 Margaret returned to England for medical treatment. Mackintosh missed her terribly. On her return, he was complaining of a sore throat and blistered tongue. Eventually he became so ill that the Mackintoshes were forced to return to London to seek medical advice. Mackintosh was diagnosed as having cancer of the tongue and, after painful radium treatment and a brief recovery, he died on 10 December 1928 at the age of sixty. After his death Margaret continued to spend her summers in France but survived her husband by only four years.

In a life marked by many ironies, two twists of fate in Mackintosh's final years are especially thought-provoking. In 1924, wartime restrictions long since lifted, Bassett-Lowke had acquired a site and was ready to commission a new house. But by this time Mackintosh, who was to have been the designer, had moved to France and Bassett-Lowke had lost touch with him. Unable to find any other British architect working in the modern manner, he approached the German Peter Behrens. 'New Ways', his completed design, is generally acknowledged to be the first modern house built in England and incorporated much of the furniture Mackintosh designed for Derngate. Then, five years later, in 1929, a group of Austrian architects obtained Mackintosh's address and wrote to invite him to Vienna, in order to celebrate his great influence on the art and architecture of their country. Unknown to them, he was already dead.

The larger ironies amount to a catalogue of 'if-onlys' and 'might-have-beens'. Wider exposure of Mackintosh's architectural work might have fostered a better understanding of his unique approach and brought him to the attention of sympathetic clients. If the war had not cut him off from his friends in Europe; if some competition success had come his way after the School of Art; if Scotland, which inspired him, had also nurtured him – British architecture might have followed a very different course.

■ ■ ■

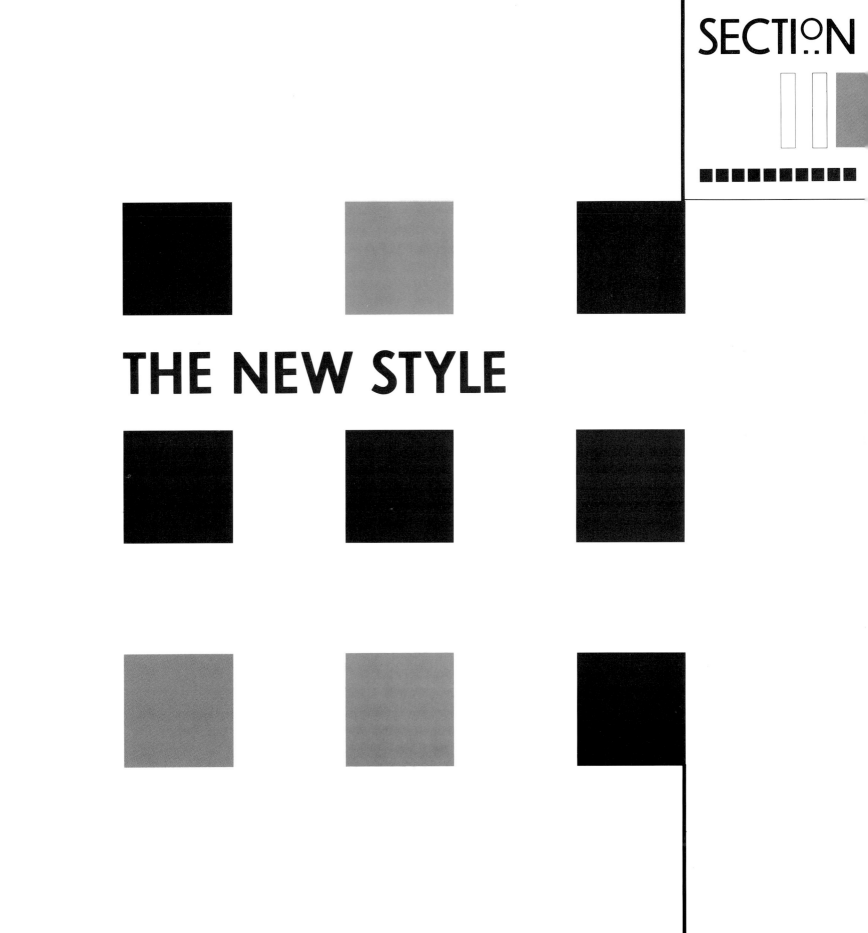

THE NEW STYLE

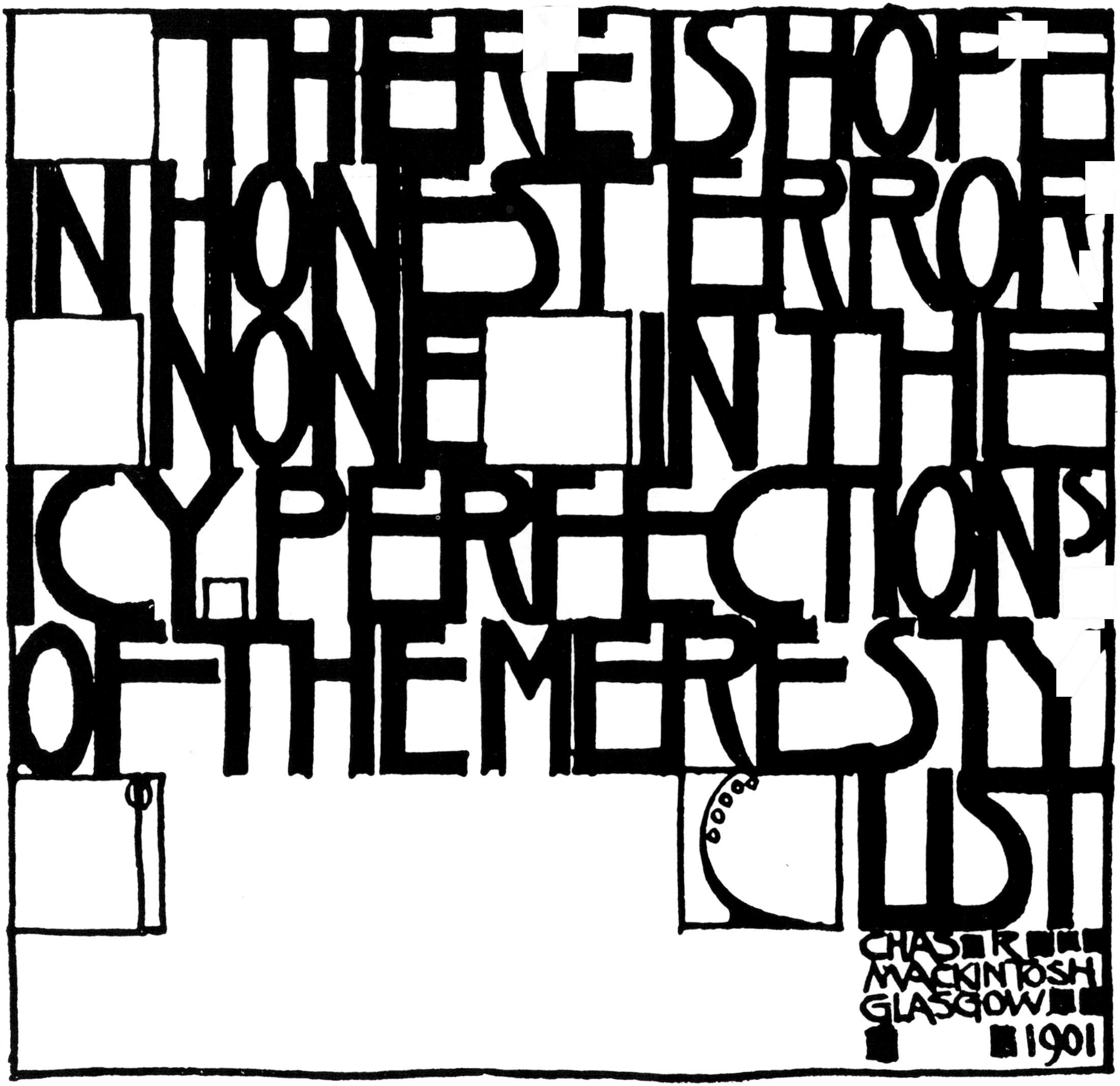

THERE IS HOPE
IN HONEST ERROR
NONE IN THE
ICY PERFECTIONS
OF THE MEREST
STYLIST

CHAS R
MACKINTOSH
GLASGOW
1901

THE NEW STYLE

Mackintosh's rooms are refined to a degree which the lives of even the artistically educated are still a long way from matching . . . they are milestones placed by a genius far ahead of us to mark the way to excellence for mankind in the future.

MUTHESIUS'S ASSESSMENT OF MACKINTOSH'S WHITE INTERIORS IN HIS BOOK *DAS ENGLISCHE HAUS* accords them the status of a work of art. The Secessionist designers of Vienna viewed Mackintosh as the prophet of a new design age and hailed him as 'the greatest since the Gothic'. More recently, architectural historians have seen Mackintosh's work as the last link in the chain of Victorian progressive thought, a reforming tradition which began with Pugin. The work of the Glasgow designers, and Mackintosh in particular, resists easy categorization. 'Art Nouveau' was never a term Mackintosh himself countenanced, and he took pains to dissociate his work from the sinuous, melting curves of Continental practitioners such as Horta and Guimard. Mackintosh was the most original member of the group centred on his native city, and the only one to achieve international stature. But the Glasgow Style was indisputably a movement with many affinities with Art Nouveau and, in some fashion, would probably have come about without his involvement.

Mackintosh's stated aim was to express old forms in a new way, to achieve a national style unencumbered by the 'props' of historical ornament. Nevertheless, his approach did not rule out

'There is Hope in Honest Error: None in the Icy Perfections of the Mere Stylist', Charles Rennie Mackintosh, Glasgow, 1901. This motto, a quotation from the architect J. D. Sedding, was first incorporated in Mackintosh's design for an invitation card for the School of Art Club meeting in 1892. This hand lettered version, which dates from 1901, displays Mackintosh's characteristic alphabet and was published in Vienna in 1902. Sedding's message, denouncing the sterility of borrowed or copied styles in favour of honest artistic endeavour, had enduring appeal for Mackintosh and The Four.

decorative or expressive elements and his 'modernity' was always conceived in the context of his Scottishness. Like Mackintosh's particular blend of old and new, the Glasgow Style was the product of diverse influences, emerging at a turning-point in the history of design and embodying many of its contradictions.

■   ■   ■

:THE: BATTLE OF THE STYLES

THE ROOTS OF MACKINTOSH'S ARCHITECTURAL APPROACH CAN BE TRACED BACK TO THE WORK AND teachings of A. W. N. Pugin (1812–1852). Pugin, a convert to Catholicism, sought to provide architecture with a moral dimension. Buildings, he believed, were a direct expression of the society which gave rise to them; 'good' architecture, therefore, could only be produced by a 'good' society, a supreme standard he found only in the buildings of the Middle Ages. Pugin's enthusiasm for the Gothic and his hatred of classical or 'pagan' architecture drew up the battle lines in the Victorian war of styles.

Pugin's theories led him to justify the grounds for good building in terms of 'honest structure' and 'truthful expression'. In the first expression of that well-known modern dictum 'form follows function', he argued that 'all ornament should consist of enrichment of the essential construction of the building' – 'decorated construction' rather than 'constructed decoration' in the Victorian architectural catchphrase. The idea that the form of a building should reflect its internal organization, that windows and doors should be placed according to practical need rather than stylistic conceit, permeated Victorian progressive thought. It was, of course, a defining characteristic of Mackintosh's work.

Pugin's radical ideas gained wider currency through the influence of the Ecclesiological Society, established in 1839 as a reforming movement within the Church of England. The work of two architect members of the society, William Butterfield and G. E. Street, demonstrated how the Gothic could be adapted to meet contemporary needs and conditions. Butterfield's churches, with their exuberant polychromatic brickwork, confirmed the Gothic as the acceptable Victorian ecclesiastical style, a convention Mackintosh would later glancingly acknowledge in his competition design for Liverpool Cathedral.

Classicism, which had dominated architecture and design in Britain since the late Renaissance, was not readily deposed. The classical orders, minutely catalogued and studied by generations of designers, amounted to a rich architectural language that formed the basis of academic teaching and practical training. Scotland had been a classical stronghold since the eighteenth century, when the work of William Adam and his more famous sons, Robert and James, was particularly influential. The Greek Revival in the early decades of the nineteenth century was expressed most powerfully in

Edinburgh, the 'Athens of the North'. In Glasgow, the leading architect in the middle years of the century was Alexander 'Greek' Thomson (1817–1875), a vehement opponent of the Gothic. The churches, villas and office buildings he designed display an original and forceful handling of classical forms, coupled with more exotic influences derived from Egypt, India and the Near East.

While Gothicists and Classicists fought their intellectual skirmishes over the moral high ground, the characteristic feature of mainstream Victorian building remained eclecticism. Inside and out, the Victorian house displayed a dizzy blend of influences: neo-rococo, Italian Renaissance, neo-Gothic, Moorish, Oriental. At the popular level, the styles of the past became a glorified dressing-up box, to be copied and applied with varying degrees of authenticity. 'The present age is distinguished from all others in having no style which can be properly called its own,' commented a 1840 guide to interior decoration. Twenty years on, the situation had only intensified.

Nineteenth-century architects were expected to acquire more than a passing familiarity with every significant historical or cultural style. Owen Jones's *The Grammar of Ornament* (1856) was the working tool of this process, codifying the eclectic approach in a comprehensive catalogue of decoration and stylistic features from around the world. The successful architect was skilled at the manipulation of historical styles, and chiefly concerned with turning out buildings in the appropriate decorative clothing.

The effect of this rampant eclecticism was to call into question the whole notion of style itself. The role of decoration or ornament in architecture, the desirability of a natural or national style freed from borrowed influences were issues to be addressed by the succeeding generation of designers.

Detail of the entrance to 'Garden Corner', Chelsea Embankment, London, refurbished by C. F. A. Voysey in 1908. 'Simplicity,' said Voysey, 'is the end, not the beginning.'

ONE OF THE MOST INFLUENTIAL FIGURES IN THE DEVELOPMENT OF DESIGN IN THE NINETEENTH CENTURY, and Pugin's intellectual descendant, was John Ruskin. Through his writings and lectures he asserted the supremacy of Nature as the source of all artistic inspiration. Like Pugin, Ruskin idealized medieval life and argued for a return to the spirit of artisanship, honest design arising naturally through the process of work. In architecture, Ruskin instructed:

The first thing to be required of a building – not, observe, the highest thing, but the first thing – is that it shall answer its purpose completely, permanently, and at the smallest expense . . . The sacrifice of any of these first requirements to external appearance is a futility and absurdity.

:THE: ARTS & CRAFTS MOVE- MENT

The upper landing at Red House, Bexleyheath, Kent, designed in 1859 by Philip Webb for William Morris. The house was decorated and furnished by Morris and his friends. The design of Red House, informal, vernacular and unpretentious, had an immense influence on domestic building during the latter part of the nineteenth century.

Unsurprisingly, Ruskin was among Mackintosh's favourite authors; *The Stones of Venice* accompanied him on his Italian tour. But it was William Morris (1834–1896) and his followers in the Arts and Crafts movement who were the first to put Ruskinian ideals into practice. Repulsed by the shoddiness and mediocrity of mass-produced goods, fired by the conviction that 'art is the expression of man's pleasure in his labour', Morris almost single-handedly brought about a revival of English craftsmanship. The printed fabrics, papers, carpets and furnishings created by his firm using old methods and traditional materials, his characteristic patterns with their rich evocation of the natural world, and his wide-ranging polemical writings and lectures exerted an immense influence on an entire generation at home and abroad.

Equally important in the development of architecture during this period was Morris's own house, completed in 1860. Red House, designed by Morris's friend and colleague Philip Webb, was one of the first English buildings directly inspired by the vernacular. An honest use of local materials – a warm red brick provided the house with its name – exposed structural elements, and the hospitably irregular L-shaped plan constituted a radical departure from the historicism of contemporary design. Predictably, when Morris came to furnish his new house he found few ready-made items to his taste, and the decorations, furniture and fittings were all designed and made by Morris, Webb and their friends. 'More a poem than a house, but admirable to live in too', in the estimation of Rossetti, Red House was a turning-point in the quest for a new style.

Like Webb, Norman Shaw was also an architect who looked to early English building for inspiration; in his case, the unassuming brick buildings from the period of Queen Anne and the early Georges. Both architects had originally trained in the office of G. E. Street; Morris had also spent time there before

■ ■ ■

Standen, Sussex, built by Philip Webb in 1882–94 as a weekend home for a solicitor, was furnished and decorated with many Morris designs. Standen's 'human quality' attracted much contemporary approval. In contrast to the claustrophobic clutter of late Victorian style, such Arts and Crafts interiors displayed a radical simplicity.

abandoning his architectural ambitions. From about 1870 onwards, as the battle of the styles fizzled out, the 'sweetness and light' of the Queen Anne style seemed to offer a way of maintaining continuity with the past, while providing the flexibility to meet modern needs.

J. J. Stevenson, a convert to the new ideas, put forward the so-called Scottish Baronial style as a substitutute for Queen Anne north of the border, a suggestion taken up in the work of architects such as James Maclaren, William Dunn and Robert Watson. Scottish Baronial was a style that harked back to the last form of Scottish building that could justifiably be termed indigenous – the fortified manors and country houses of the sixteenth and seventeenth centuries. Rugged, plain, and unpretentiously constructed in stone with roughcast exteriors, such buildings nevertheless had a certain dramatic appeal, with their turrets, crow-stepped gables and stout chimneys.

Morris had advocated a simplicity and integrity in design which transcended superficial stylistic concerns. 'Have nothing in your houses which you do not know to be useful or believe to be beautiful' was his famous 'golden rule'. Some of his followers in what became known as the Arts and Crafts movement came to see style as virtually an irrelevance. 'Art is not a special sauce applied to ordinary cooking; it is the cooking itself if it is good,' asserted W. R. Lethaby.

W. R. Lethaby (1857–1931) was a key figure in the groups which sprang up in the wake of Morris and his immediate circle. Trained as an architect in Norman Shaw's office, he helped to set up the Art Workers' Guild and was later the President of the Arts and Crafts Exhibition Society. From 1893 he was a member of the Society for the Protection of Ancient Buildings, an organization founded by Morris to prevent the common nineteenth-century practice of 'restoring' old monuments and churches so invasively that their historical character was all but lost. The Society was also responsible for gathering and publishing a great deal of information about old building techniques and materials, an invaluable resource for those interested in reviving vernacular forms.

Lethaby's book *Architecture, Mysticism and Myth* (1892) had such a profound effect on Mackintosh that he borrowed virtually the complete text of his 1893 lecture from it. In this dense and complex work, Lethaby approached the vexed question of style by investigating the ancient origins of architectural form and examining the role of symbolism in building. If there were universal symbols, common to all cultures, in which the meaning of a building could be invested, then such ornamentation would not be incompatible with modern design and could provide a vehicle for preserving continuity with the past. The result would be a truly modern form of decoration, not the sort of stylistic imitation whereby banks, theatres, and churches masqueraded as Greek temples. In other words, it would not be necessary to copy an antique temple façade, merely to express the underlying meaning of its features. The column, for example, in its reference to timber construction, could be seen as symbolic of the tree or even, more fundamentally, the life force itself.

In Mackintosh's rendition of Lethaby's ideas, modern architecture should be 'designs by living men for living men', expressing 'fresh realization of sacred fact – or personal broodings – of skill – of joy in nature in grace – of form and gladness of colour'. Mackintosh had a highly developed sense of symbolism, and both the structural form of his buildings and the decorative motifs he employed – the squares, the abstracted rosebuds, insects and plant forms – display his application of these ideas to powerful effect.

King Cophetua and the Beggar Maid, **Edward Burne-Jones (1833–98). The heightened realism of the work of the Pre-Raphaelite painters, together with their romantic subject matter and use of symbolism, were formative influences on the development of Mackintosh's artistic imagination. Pre-Raphaelite reproductions were on display in Mackintosh's first studio.**

C. F. A. Voysey was another architect who was to have immense influence on the development of the Mackintosh style. A member of the Art Workers' Guild, one of the innumerable societies that comprised the Arts and Crafts movement as a whole, Voysey took to heart Morris's emphasis on material and technique.

It seems to me that to produce any satisfactory work of art we must acquire a complete knowledge of our material and be thoroughly masters of the craft to be employed in its production . . . go to Nature direct for inspiration and guidance. Then we are at once relieved from restrictions of style or period, and can live and work in the present with laws revealing always fresh possibilities.

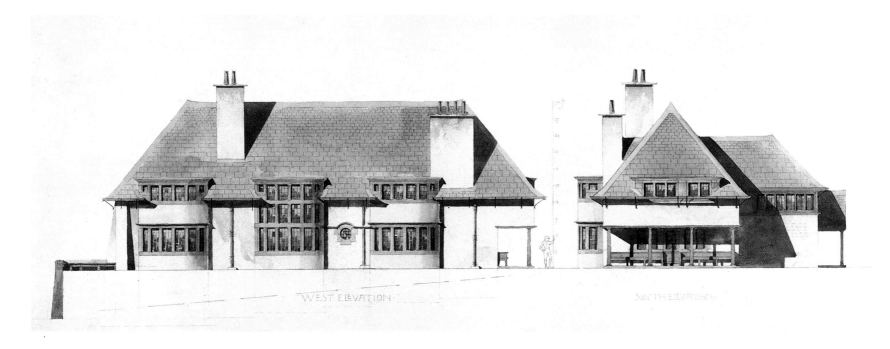

WEST ELEVATION · *SOUTH ELEVATION*

The writings, architectural work and interior designs of the English architect C. F. A. Voysey struck a chord with Mackintosh. Voysey's vernacular yet modern designs, such as 'Broadleys', Lake Windermere, Cumbria (1898), proved highly influential in their apparent 'stylelessness'.

Voysey's words, recorded in *The Studio* in 1893, found a ready audience in Mackintosh. Direct exposure to Voysey's work came via the Arts and Crafts Society Exhibition in 1896, where Mackintosh was able to assess at first hand the work of this versatile designer.

Voysey's output was almost entirely in the sphere of domestic building. His simple vernacular houses, with their low roofs, sheltering eaves and plain walls, and his interiors, stripped of ornament and furnished with forthright pieces of his own design, were revolutionary in their 'stylelessness' and were to prove highly influential in twentieth-century urban development.

Mackintosh began his architectural career at a time of great promise and potential. The progressive ideas of Morris, Norman Shaw, Voysey and Lethaby provided the intellectual context for his work, ideological developments which also inspired the leaders of the new art movement on the Continent. As his first lecture of 1891 reveals, Mackintosh had absorbed enough of this thinking to adopt the Scottish Baronial as his own point of reference, a native building tradition of crow-stepped gables, angle turrets, dormers and steeply pitched roofs; while study of Ruskin had confirmed his own belief in the ultimate inspiration of Nature. From Morris and his followers, too, he had derived a notion of architecture as 'the synthesis of the fine arts, the commune of all the crafts'. Yet Mackintosh's allegiance to the Arts and Crafts school of thought was only one aspect of his development; other sources of influence help to explain why he would never be admitted to the fold.

■ ■ ■

Trees and Swallows, **a fabric design by C. F. A. Voysey. Voysey was inspired directly from nature. He produced many designs for fabrics, carpets and wallpapers in the latter part of his career.**

THE AES- THETES

OTHER POWERFUL INFLUENCES WHICH MADE THEIR IMPACT ON MACKINTOSH'S DEVELOPMENT AS A designer came from a quarter whose pursuit of art for its own sake was fundamentally opposed to the social concerns of the Arts and Crafts movement. The 'Aesthetic' movement of the late nineteenth century did not subscribe to the notion that art was a means of social betterment. Morris, with his socialist ideals, believed that art could be a way of improving and uplifting everyday life. 'I do not want art for a few, any more than I want education for a few, or freedom for a few . . . ' he proclaimed in one of his lectures. The Aesthetes, on the other hand, set the artist apart from society, with a duty only to art itself. Society might not understand, or approve, or find the results relevant or useful; art could only be judged in its own terms.

These philosophical differences inevitably led to hostilies between the two camps. The Aesthetes, who numbered Whistler and Beardsley among their leading lights, were popularly derided for their excessive sensibility, moral 'decadence' and elitism. W. S. Gilbert's *Patience* satirized the 'greenery-yallery, Grosvenor Gallery' young men, with their languid refinement and morbid melancholy: 'Though the Philistines may jostle, you will rank as an apostle in the high aesthetic band,/If you walk down Piccadilly with a poppy or a lily in your medieval hand.' Even Morris took pains to dissociate himself from the 'dingy bilious looking yellow-green', a fashionable paintwork shade in Aesthetic circles.

The Aesthetic movement had been given particular impetus by the discovery of Japanese prints in the early 1860s. Trading links with Japan were reopened in the middle of the century, and woodcuts by such masters as Hokusai began to find their way to Europe. The story, which may be apocryphal, has it that such prints were originally used as humble wrappings for imported Japanese porcelain, or 'Nankin china'. In any event, the effect on European artists was electrifying. The linearity of the Japanese prints, the stylization of nature, the apparent delight in the pure aesthetic pleasure of colour and form offered a new direction for artistic development, a way of breaking free from the past.

Woodblock print illustrating a poem by Sanji Hitoshi, Daimyo meditating on his lost love, *from a series begun by the 'ukiyoe' artist Hokusai (1760–1849) in 1835. The discovery of such prints by Western artists in the middle of the nineteenth century provoked an intense interest in Japanese art and culture.*

*For shipping magnate
Frederick Leyland, Whistler
transformed The Peacock
Room into* Harmony in Blue
and Gold. *Whistler's use of
colour to generate
atmosphere and heighten
sensibility was highly
provocative.*

Whistler and Beardsley, in particular, were highly influenced by Oriental art and became keen collectors, as was the Pre-Raphaelite Dante Gabriel Rossetti. It is not insignificant that both Pre-Raphaelite reproductions and Japanese prints were displayed in Mackintosh's first studio.

By the late nineteenth century the craze for Japanese art and design was at its height. Japanese flower arranging, the Japanese house and garden, Japanese artefacts of all descriptions were the focus of much attention, comment and emulation. More popularly, *Japonaiserie* – furnishings and decorative objects with a Japanese flavour – was all the rage, and the familiar motifs of the sunflower or peacock feather came to summarize the style. Arthur Lasenby Liberty's new furnishings store, which purveyed imported Oriental goods, as well as the paisley print dress fabric favoured by aesthetically minded women, was the Mecca for devotees. In *Punch*, George du Maurier's poem *Oscar* lampooned the Japanese-influenced aesthete as 'quite too consummately utter, as well as too utterly quite'.

'The greatest aesthete of them all', in the estimation of Max Beerbohm, was the designer and architect E. W. Godwin, who created interiors for Whistler and Wilde. The Aesthetes, through their interest in symbol and subjective experience, used colour in an associative way, to excite feeling and generate mood and atmosphere in the interior. Going into Whistler's bright yellow breakfast room was compared to walking into an egg; for Wilde, Godwin conceived 'a masterpiece in pearl', a dining-room entirely in white and muted shades of grey. Whistler's famous transformation of The Peacock Room for shipping magnate Frederick Leyland involved completely covering the walls with turquoise and gold peacocks, a decorative effort of some eight months: Whistler called it 'Harmony in Blue and Gold'. His own paintings, with their symbolic reliance on only one or two colours, aroused much controversy. When Ruskin described one of Whistler's works as 'flinging a pot of paint in the public's face', Whistler sued for libel. He won the derisory damages of one farthing; the legal costs ruined him.

Aubrey Beardsley (1872–1898) was an equally provocative figure. His illustrations for the periodical *The Yellow Book* (first published in 1894), for Wilde's *Salome* and Pope's *Rape of the Lock* won him much notoriety through their erotic, sinister and grotesque imagery. The taut, curving lines of his style, the bold flat areas of black and white contrasted with intricate detail are an obvious influence on the style of the Glasgow designers.

The Studio, first published in 1893, provided the vehicle for introducing such work to Mackintosh and his circle. The first issue of this avant-garde magazine included a commentary on Beardsley as well as a reproduction of Jan Toorop's mystical work, *The Three Brides*. This strange painting, an allegory of the Church, seems to have struck a particularly powerful chord with The Four. A Scottish quarterly, *Evergreen*, which appeared in 1895 and ran for only a year, provided another strand of influence in its championing of a Celtic artistic revival.

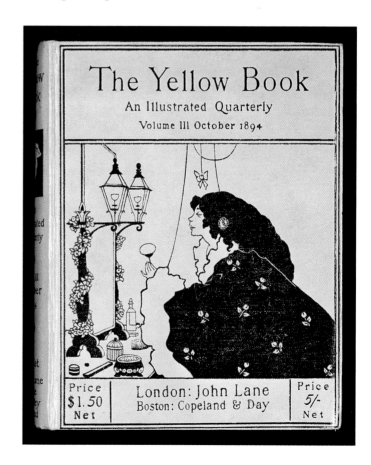

The avante-garde illustrated quarterly The Yellow Book **was first published in 1894 and eventually achieved a wide and influential circulation throughout Britain and Europe. Works by Herbert MacNair, Margaret and Frances Macdonald, including the latter's** Ill Omen **and** The Sleeping Princess**, were illustrated in 1896 volumes of the periodical.**

The impact of such influences owed much to timing. The appearance of *The Studio* coincided with Mackintosh and MacNair's introduction to the Macdonald sisters and the inception of The Four. This formative period, when Mackintosh's graphic interests were at their height, and his opportunities to build still in the future, found him most receptive to the new imagery. A few years later, the work shown by The Four at the Arts and Crafts Society Exhibition in 1896 clearly revealed its debt to the art of Japan, Beardsley's illustrative technique, and Toorop's symbolism. Here were eerie female figures with attentuated, stylized bodies, abstracted natural and organic forms, swirling patterns of lines, and overall an atmosphere of brooding melancholy – everything, in fact, most suggestive to the worthies of the Arts and Crafts Society of the decadent, unhealthy world of the *demi-monde*.

■ ■ ■

:THE: GLAS- :G:W STYLE

THERE IS HOPE IN HONEST ERROR: NONE IN THE ICY PERFECTION OF THE MERE STYLIST.' THE QUOTATION, from an address given by the architect J. D. Sedding to the Arts and Crafts Society, was the rallying call of the newly formed Four. Little more than a decade later, their work was the nucleus of a movement which embraced all the arts. 'Nowhere has the modern movement of art been entered upon more seriously than at Glasgow; the church, the school, the house, the restaurant, the shop, the poster, the book, with its printing, illustrating and binding, have all come under the spell of the new influence.' This comment, which appeared in *The Studio* in 1907, effectively summarizes the scope of the Glasgow Style and the artistic vitality of the city in which it emerged. As Mackintosh found to his cost, Glasgow's receptiveness to original ideas was not to last, but for this short period around the turn of the century the new art flourished there.

A growing interest in the decorative arts accompanied Glasgow's booming prosperity in the late nineteenth century. In the words of David Brett: 'Glasgow was ripe for an avant-garde'. The 'Glasgow Boys' had done much to establish this favourable climate, and their international recognition was the source of some civic pride; the studio of W. Y. MacGregor was a gathering place where the like-minded met to discuss ideas. The dealer Alex Reid was instrumental in encouraging local patrons to invest in the work of the Glasgow Boys; many also collected the work of French Impressionists, which Reid introduced to the city in 1892. Inevitably, in the tight-knit world of Glasgow's cultural life, Mackintosh became acquainted with many of the artistic fraternity and familiar with their work.

The Glasgow School of painting can be counted a significant influence on the development of the Glasgow Style. The tendency, particularly evident in the work of George Henry, E. A. Hornel and David Gauld, towards the surface qualities of colour and decoration at the expense of narrative or realism, never attained the abstraction of modern art, but did anticipate the work of European symbolists such as Klimt. Paintings such as *The Druids: Bringing in the Mistletoe* (1889) by George Henry and E. A. Hornel must have held Mackintosh in their sway, with their rich areas of colour and Celtic imagery. In such works, the line between fine and decorative art was blurred; the point of cross-over proved fertile ground in which the Glasgow Style could grow and flourish.

Francis ('Fra') Newbery, newly appointed Director of the School of Art, was a pivotal figure in the emergence of the new style. Under his direction, the School, with its concentration of artists, designers and craftworkers, became a focus for artistic endeavour and experiment. Newbery had trained as a painter and was fully acquainted with contemporary developments in the Arts and Crafts movement. His introduction of Mackintosh and MacNair to the Macdonald sisters was not an isolated insight. In 1889 Newbery married a former student, Jessie Rowat, who went on to establish an embroidery department at the School and develop her own highly original and well-regarded style. He promoted work of other young students, including Jessie King, whose long career encompassed wallpaper, textile and jewellery design as well as the book covers and illustrations for which she is better known.

George Walton (1867–1933), the younger brother of E. A. Walton, one of the Glasgow Boys, is generally regarded as an important forerunner of the new style. In 1888, at the age of twenty-one, Walton abandoned his job as a bank clerk and set up as a designer and decorator on the strength of a single commission: to decorate a smoking room at Miss Cranston's Argyle Street Tea Rooms. Six years later he had built up a considerable reputation, chiefly through his designs for wallpaper and stencilled decoration, some of which prefigured the work of Continental practitioners of

In a Japanese Garden, **by George Henry. Japanese art had an immense impact on the cultural life of Glasgow. Glasgow 'Boys' George Henry and E. A. Hornel spent a year in Japan (1893–4) and conveyed their enthusiastic impressions to lecture audiences on their return. From woodblock prints to flower arranging, from Japanese architecture to the form of the kimono, all aspects of Japanese life were avidly studied by Mackintosh and his circle.**

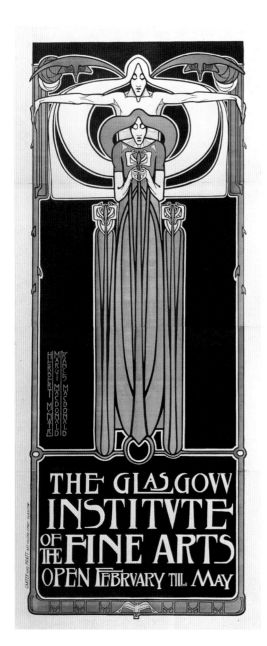

The design of posters provided a fruitful medium for The Four to express their ideas. This poster for the Glasgow Institute for the Fine Arts dates from 1898 and was the result of a collaboration between Frances and Margaret Macdonald and Herbert MacNair.

Art Nouveau such as Horta. In 1896 Walton was commissioned to furnish Miss Cranston's new venture at Buchanan Street, with Mackintosh executing wall decorations under his direction. The following year Mackintosh also designed furniture for the enlarged and refurbished Argyle Street premises, while Walton took responsibility for decorations and fittings and retained overall design control. The tea-room commissions were to prove one of the most enduring outlets for the Glasgow Style.

Despite their collaboration on the tea-room schemes, Walton and Mackintosh evolved their approaches independently of each other. Walton left Glasgow in 1897, setting up in London and, a year later, in York, where he enjoyed considerable commercial success. If his work retained hints of the Glasgow Style, it was in a form more obviously in tune with the tastes of the Arts and Crafts movement and consequently more saleable in the English market.

In 1897, the 'Mac' group (*The Studio*'s nickname for The Four) were visited by Gleeson White, the only English critic to have formed a favourable impression of the Glasgow designers at the 1896 exhibition. Of their work, White had written:

Probably nothing in the gallery has provoked more decided censure that these various exhibits; and that fact alone should cause a thoughtful observer of art to pause before he joins the opponents. If the said artists do not come very prominently forward as leaders of a school of design peculiarly their own, we shall be very much mistaken. The probability would seem to be that those who laugh at them to-day will be eager to eulogize them a few years hence.

Notwithstanding his enthusiasm, Gleeson White fully expected to encounter a dreary band of aesthetes and was particularly astonished to discover that the Macdonald sisters proved to be 'two laughing comely girls, scarce out of their teens' rather than a pair of middle-aged spinsters. The Macdonald sisters, Frances and Margaret, were, in fact, rather older than Gleeson White had estimated, but their cheerful outlook dispelled any notion he might have entertained of 'unhealthy' or morbid Aestheticism. The sisters were English-born daughters of a consulting engineer; the family had moved to Glasgow from Staffordshire in the late 1880s. Both began to attend drawing classes at the School of Art in 1890, when Margaret was twenty-six and Frances seventeen. By 1893 their work must have been sufficiently distinctive for Newbery to have made his inspired connection; after this date, The Four evolved their characteristic approach more or less together.

According to G. and C. Larners' *The Glasgow Style*, Mackintosh's design for a diploma awarded by the Glasgow School of Art Club constitutes the first example of Glasgow's version of Art Nouveau. The stylized form of an apple tree, branches extending out at right angles to provide a taut framework for the design, was a motif readily adopted by the other members of the group. But originality was not confined to Mackintosh. Frances, of the two sisters, had perhaps greater imaginative powers, and her 1893 watercolour *Ill Omen* introduced the powerful image of a flight of swooping birds to The Four's repertoire; Margaret, on the other hand, was more assured and more able to adapt her work. Both sisters excelled at embroidery and metalwork; their embroidered panels and mirror frames revealed the inherent potential of both media as vehicles of the new style. Herbert MacNair was an accomplished graphic artist, and some of his early furniture designs, such as a cabinet of 1895 and a smoker's cabinet illustrated in *The Studio* in 1897, were more radical than the work Mackintosh was producing at that time.

MacNair's work was featured alongside that of Talwin Morris (1865–1911) in the second of the two *Studio* articles Gleeson White devoted to the Glasgow designers. Morris, a close friend of The Four and an early collector of their work, had arrived in Glasgow in 1893 after securing the post of Art Director at the publisher Blackie's. In this role Morris was able to bring the new style to a wider

The Sleeping Princess, **Frances Macdonald, 1895. The watercolour, with its haunting imagery, appeared in** The Yellow Book**, no. 11, 1896. The beaten lead frame is inscribed: 'Love if thy tresses be so dark/How dark those hidden eyes must be'.**

audience; his designs for book covers made skilful use of graphic motifs developed by The Four. He won greater critical attention for his metalwork, however, particularly for his finely made door furniture and jewellery in the idiom of the new style.

The early opportunities that arose to put the new style into practice testify to the interwoven nature of Glasgow's cultural life. The most famous example is Newbery's role in securing for Mackintosh his greatest commission, the design of the School of Art. But Newbery probably also introduced his protégé to William Davidson, prominent local patron of the work of the Glasgow Boys. Mackintosh produced designs and furniture for the Davidson family home, Gladsmuir, between 1894 and 1897, an involvement which was ultimately to lead to the commission of Windyhill for the Davidsons' son William (junior) and his family. Another significant introduction came through the agency of Talwin Morris, who suggested Mackintosh as a suitable architect to his employer Walter Blackie: the result was to be The Hill House. Again, when the parents of the Macdonald sisters moved to Dunglass Castle (previously the home of Talwin Morris), Mackintosh was inevitably involved in the remodelling of the drawing-room; it included one of the earliest examples of his characteristic fireplace designs. Mackintosh also created a number of fireplaces, a settle and some light fittings for the Rowat family, parents of Jessie, the wife of Francis Newbery.

Newbery's efforts on behalf of the young designers ensured that their work was exhibited at every available opportunity. Local uproar greeted their first exposure at the 1894 Art Club exhibition at the School of Art. The following year a provocative exhibition at the School attracted European attention and transferred to Liège. In 1902, following The Four's triumph at Vienna two years previously, Newbery was asked to organize the Scottish section at the International Exhibition of Modern Decorative Art at Turin; the exhibitors amounted to a roll-call of School of Art students, past and present: the Mackintoshes, Frances and Herbert MacNair, Newbery's wife Jessie, Jessie King and her future husband E. A. Taylor, Ann Macbeth from the embroidery department and Peter Wylie Davidson from the metalwork department, among others.

Newbery placed Mackintosh in charge of the design of the Scottish section at Turin, with a cavernous gallery lit by large windows at his disposal. Mackintosh transformed this unpromising setting into a sequence of three airy, cool spaces, imbued with a sense of tranquillity. Narrow stencilled linen panels which Mackintosh created *in situ* divided the space into three display bays and provided an element of graphic punctuation. Windows screened with fine muslin, white painted woodwork, and whitewashed upper walls and ceiling formed a pristine backdrop for the subtle colours of the

THAT·WALL·OF·STONE·THAT·SHUT·THE·FLOWERS·AND·TREES UP·WITH·THE·SKY·AND·TREBLED·ALL·THE·BEAUTY·

Illustration by Jessie M. King for The Defence of Guinevere *by William Morris. While a student at the Glasgow School of Art, Jessie King created an illuminated history of the school on vellum, which was buried under the foundation stone of the new building.*

The Heart of the Rose, Margaret Macdonald Mackintosh, 1901 (ABOVE). **This beautiful gesso panel was created for** *The Rose Boudoir,* **the room setting designed, furnished and decorated by the Mackintoshes at the International Exhibition of Modern Decorative Arts, Turin, 1902. The sweeping, embracing curves, roseheads in full bloom and imagery of fertility and fruition suggest the ripeness of creativity.**

■ ■ ■

This pair of embroidered panels (RIGHT) *by Margaret Macdonald Mackintosh, worked for* The Hill House, *1902, shows how readily the new style adapted to different media. Similar panels were shown at Vienna in 1900 and Turin in 1902. The Blackie children nicknamed the subjects the 'skinny ladies'.*

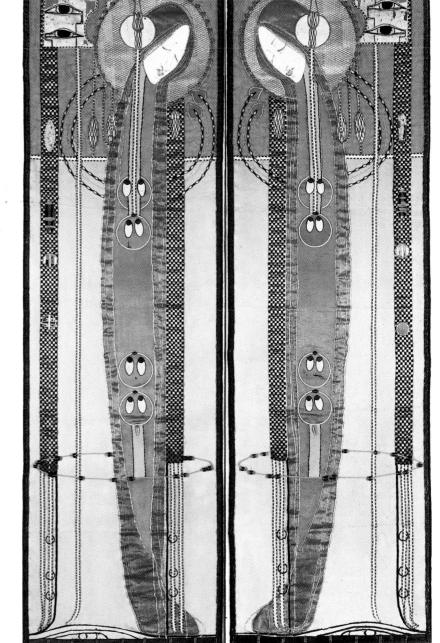

decorative work. The first bay, devoted to the work of Mackintosh and his wife, was in two parts: a 'Rose Boudoir' featuring painted gesso, beaten silver and needlework panels by Margaret, and pendant light fittings and furniture by Mackintosh; and an adjacent area where architectural drawings were displayed. *The Studio* found the ensemble to be 'the epitome of work of an architect and art-worker labouring together as co-partners in the same scheme'.

The second bay at Turin was furnished as a writing room by Frances and Herbert MacNair, with grey, gold and white decoration and a stencilled frieze. The third displayed various contributions from the other exhibitors, ranging from Jessie Newbery's embroidery and E. A Taylor's furniture to Jessie King's book illustrations (one of her book covers won a gold medal).

Mary Sturrock, Newbery's daughter, later recalled an incident during the setting up of the exhibition which encapsulates Mackintosh's attitude of perfectionism. Once everything had been assembled and arranged precisely to the architect's satisfaction, Newbery proposed ordering some flowers as a finishing touch. Mackintosh objected vociferously and insisted on going out into the countryside to find just the right twigs and branches to create the appropriately sparse and artistic arrangement.

The impact created by the Scottish section heightened Mackintosh's European reputation. The Mackintoshes' work won a diploma of honour and they received, and accepted, invitations to exhibit in Budapest and Moscow. Virtually an entire issue of *Deutsche Kunst und Dekoration* was devoted to a review of their work. The year before Turin, at the Glasgow International Exhibition of 1901, there were indications of the new style's progress into the commercial mainstream. Wylie and Lochhead, a Glaswegian firm of cabinet-makers, exhibited a furnished pavilion in the Glasgow style, which included room settings designed by E. A. Taylor, George Logan and John Ednie, whose work was directly inspired by Mackintosh. Some of this work was shown again at Turin in 1902.

The warm Continental welcome for Mackintosh and his circle did not bring about a change of heart back home. English critics did not cease their tirades against the new art of the Scottish designers; only *The Studio* remained a loyal supporter. In 1907, nine years after Gleeson White had died, its endorsement of Mackintosh remained unequivocal: 'No artist owes less to tradition than does Mackintosh; as an originator he is supreme.'

Mackintosh was the guiding light of the new style, and its fortunes were inextricably linked to his own. Walton and MacNair both left Glasgow in 1898, and the Larners make the suggestion that both designers had come to the conclusion that Mackintosh's creative genius would inevitably overshadow any work they could produce in the city. Jessie King and E. A. Taylor left in 1908; Talwin Morris died in 1911. Mackintosh, as we have seen, began to encounter serious difficulties after 1906; by 1908, when the MacNairs returned from Liverpool, the art school closed and their income exhausted, the future of new art in Glasgow looked bleak indeed.

The dining room at Maison Horta (1898–1901), designed by Victor Horta. Horta was skilled at manipulating light and shade; sinuous lines and organic curves were used to give the impression of fluidity in the interior.

NEW: ART IN EUROPE

ART NOUVEAU APPEARED IN EUROPE AT ABOUT THE SAME TIME AS ITS BRITISH MANIFESTATION, THE Glasgow Style, and had a life of equal brevity. But, where progressive trends in design and architecture came to a virtual stop in Britain after the turn of the century, the Modern movement as a whole went on to flourish in Europe and define the entire nature of twentieth-century artistic development.

The new style first appeared in Brussels in 1893, in the work of Victor Horta (1861–1947) and Henry van de Velde (1863–1957). Inspired by William Morris in their quest to break free from historical tradition, these architects evolved the characteristic fluid, melting curves and organic references of the style. Before long, Van de Velde's work was taken up by a Parisian art dealer, Samuel Bing, who had accurately anticipated the spirit of the times. Paris was enthralled by the new style (which took its name from Bing's shop) and its influence rapidly spread throughout the decorative

Secession House (RIGHT),
the exhibition space and
headquarters of the radical
group of Viennese artists and
architects known as the
Secession, was designed by
J. M. Olbrich in 1898.

Staircase (LEFT) from the
Post Office Savings Bank,
Vienna (1904–6), designed by
Otto Wagner. Wagner was a
leading exponent of
functionalism, principles
enshrined in this building,
one of the first examples of
modern architecture in
Europe.

arts. The German version of Art Nouveau, *Jugendstil*, was equally quickly established, and by the turn of the century few European centres were untouched by the movement.

The style, particularly its wilder excesses, was vilified in England. The undoubted similarities between some aspects of Art Nouveau and the Glasgow Style provided the excuse to tar both movements with the same brush. Yet both northern and Continental versions of the new art, which had their significant differences, appear to have emerged quite distinctly, without much reference to each other. The parallels with the Glasgow Style were stronger, and the influences more entwined, in the case of the other new movement in art, the Viennese Secession.

The Secession comprised a group of artists and architects, including Gustav Klimt, J. M. Olbrich, Josef Hoffman and Koloman Moser, who broke away from Vienna's conservative Academy of Arts in 1897; the headquarters and exhibition space for the group, the Secession House, was designed by

57

Lacquered metal mesh baskets by Josef Hoffmann, co-founder of the Vienna Secession and Wiener Werkstätte. 'As long as our towns, our homes, our rooms, our utensils, our clothing, our language and our feelings are unable to express the spirit of our times in a simple, sober and beautiful way, we will have fallen short of our ancestors. . .' proclaimed the designers of the Vienna school in the Arbeitsprogramm *of 1905.*

Olbrich in 1898. Like many of the practitioners of Art Nouveau elsewhere in Europe, the Secessionists were also inspired by William Morris and the English Arts and Crafts movement. The Wiener Werkstätte, a craft studio that Secessionist members Hoffman and Moser went on to found in 1903, embodied many Arts and Crafts ideals – its expressed aims were to revive craft skills, dispense with the distinction between the fine and decorative arts, and challenge the mediocrity of mass-produced or industrialized goods.

The work of the Austrian designers was more robust, sober and practical than the sinuous flights of fancy associated with French or Belgian Art Nouveau. Hoffman's adoption of the square as a decorative motif was already evident in work he exhibited at the Munich Secessionist Exhibition in 1899, and the new movement was well under way by 1900, when the work of The Four was first exhibited. The work of the Glasgow School of painters had been shown widely in Europe ever since

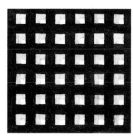

Geometric design by Josef Hoffmann (ABOVE), *c. 1930. In 1902 Mackintosh wrote to Hoffmann: 'Your aim from the beginning must be that every object is created for a specific purpose and a specific place. . .many years of hard work earnest hard work – by the leaders of the Modern Movement will be required before all obstacles are removed.'*

Armchair for the Urkersdorf Sanatorium (RIGHT), *designed by Koloman Moser, co-founder of the Vienna Secession and Wienner Werkstätte. Furniture by Mackintosh, exhibited at the Secessionist Exhibition Vienna in 1900, had an electrifying effect on the Austrian designers: 'The structure is apparent everywhere, the form is as rigorous and ample as possible. The curved line follows the structure of the frame, a nervous rigidity petrifies the shapes into almost primitive forms that stare at us with a mysterious look.'*

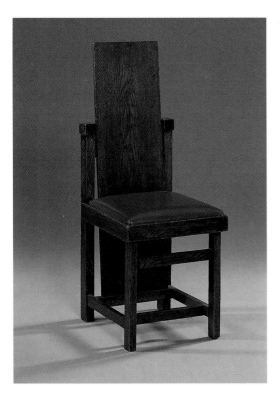

Chair for the Larkin Company canteen, Buffalo, New York, designed by Frank Lloyd Wright, 1904. Influenced by the Arts and Crafts movement and by features of traditional Japanese construction, Wright went on to create his own distinctive style and become the leading American architect of the twentieth century.

their first exposure in Munich in 1893, but it is not clear precisely how the invitation to The Four originally came about.

At any event, Mackintosh was rapturously received by the Austrian designers at the 8th Secessionist Exhibition in Vienna in 1900. To the Secessionists, here was confirmation of the direction they were seeking; for Mackintosh, contact with the vital new movement was exhilarating. The purity of Mackintosh's white rooms supported Hoffmann's own artistic intentions and gave fresh impetus to the movement as a whole. Similarities between the work of Hoffman and Mackintosh must have been striking to most observers. There is no hard evidence that either knew of the other's work prior to this date, although some critics believe the four-square motif which became such a feature of Austrian design must have originated with Mackintosh.

It is clear that, to these progressive European designers, the simplicity and rectilinear nature of Mackintosh's work represented an exciting and significant departure from the early phase of Art Nouveau. Much later, Professor (Sir) Niklaus Pevsner acknowledged this transitional role:

> Here was the wilfulness and irregularity of Art Nouveau handled with an exquisite finesse previously unknown. But here was also a sense of slender, erect verticals and smooth, unbroken surfaces which might well serve as a weapon to defeat Art Nouveau ... Mackintosh, alone ... could be a witness for the defence and for the prosecution of both Art Nouveau and anti-Art Nouveau.

Elsewhere, Pevsner likens Mackintosh to a European Frank Lloyd Wright; the two architects were almost exactly contemporary and shared many sources of inspiration.

From these strands of influence and development which came together so powerfully around the turn of the century, it is possible to see that there are grounds for many differing interpretations of Mackintosh and his role in the Glasgow Style. Effectively, he was indeed the last of the great Victorian designers, since the ideas he was developing passed on to a new generation in Europe without ever coming to fruition on home ground. His approach undoubtedly grew out of the context of Art Nouveau, but at the same time implied its demise. Profoundly artistic and visionary within the terms he set himself, the 'style' Mackintosh created ultimately began and ended with his own work.

THE ART OF SPACE

THE ART OF SPACE

The architect . . . depends very greatly for his success upon a kind of instinct, a synthesis, or integration of myriads of details and circumstances of which he cannot be directly very conscious but the appreciation of which makes the master in every profession.

M ACKINTOSH, COMPOSING A SPEECH ON THE SUBJECT OF 'SEEMLINESS', PRESENTED A SUMMARY OF HIS entire approach. Elsewhere in the notes for the same lecture, he states: 'The artist cannot attain to mastery in his art unless he is endowed in the highest degree with the faculty of invention.'

Mackintosh's unique powers of artistic imagination and his ability to conceive every detail in its relation to the whole are amply demonstrated in the small number of buildings which comprise his creative output. This chapter focuses on the best examples of his work, the projects over which he was able to exert most complete control and which express his ideas to the full. As well as his masterpiece, the School of Art, these include Windyhill and The Hill House, the interiors of his own homes at 120 Mains Street and 78 Southpark Avenue, the Willow Tea Rooms and, finally, Derngate, Northampton.

In these few works, Mackintosh unquestionably proved himself to be a master of the art of space.

The facade of the Glasgow School of Art is dominated by great north-facing windows, which flood the studio interiors with the constant even levels of light essential for painting. Reflected in the glass are wrought-iron brackets – 'the most discussed window brackets in history' – which serve to brace the first-floor windows.

Their abstracted shapes, portraying seeds, stamens and flower-buds, provide a symbolic expression of the purpose and ideals of the School of Art and serve to enrich an otherwise resolutely plain elevation. Imagery of growth, ripening and fruition is appropriate for an institution dedicated to art education.

The Glasgow School of Art

167 Renfrew Street, Glasgow
Client: Governors of the School of Art
First phase: 1897–9 Second phase: 1907–09

■ ■ ■

The Competition

:THE:
GLAS-
:G⋮OW
SCH8L
⋮F ART

B Y THE LATE 1880S, GLASGOW'S SCHOOL OF ART HAD OUTGROWN ITS CRAMPED QUARTERS IN THE Corporation Galleries in Rose Street, its rapid expansion due in part to the energetic directorship of Francis Newbery. Discussions began to take place about ways of raising money for a new building. Eventually, in 1895, ten years after Newbery's appointment, the Governors of the School were offered £10,000 ($15,500) by the Bellahouston Bequest Fund; £6,000 ($9,300) of which was intended for the purchase of a site in Renfrew Street, the remainder conditional on being matched by a further sum of £6,000 ($9,300) to be raised by the Governors.

Donations by the Governors, local firms and civic authorities had brought the total up to £21,000 ($32,550) by early 1896. A committee was formed to devise rules for a limited architectural competition for the design of 'a plain building' costing £14,000 ($21,700); five per cent of the cost was set aside as the fee for the winning competitor. Newbery was asked to specify the extent of accommodation required and advise on the size and type of windows and the nature of artificial light.

The north facade of the School of Art on Renfrew Street is an asymmetrical composition, with windows of varying sizes corresponding to the differing scale of the studios they light. The School was built in two stages. The first phase, completed in 1899, comprised the portion of the building running from the east wall to a point just past the entrance. The western half was completed in 1909.

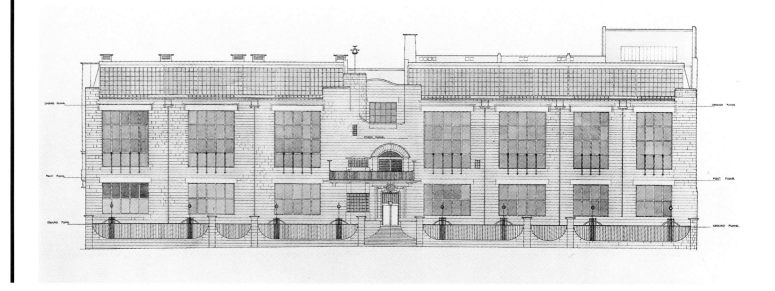

The entrance to the School of Art. The doors hang from the central tree-like post and swing in opposite directions. Below the square windows set in each door are a pair of glass inserts in the form of leaves, flanking a wooden stem which ends in the shape of a seed.

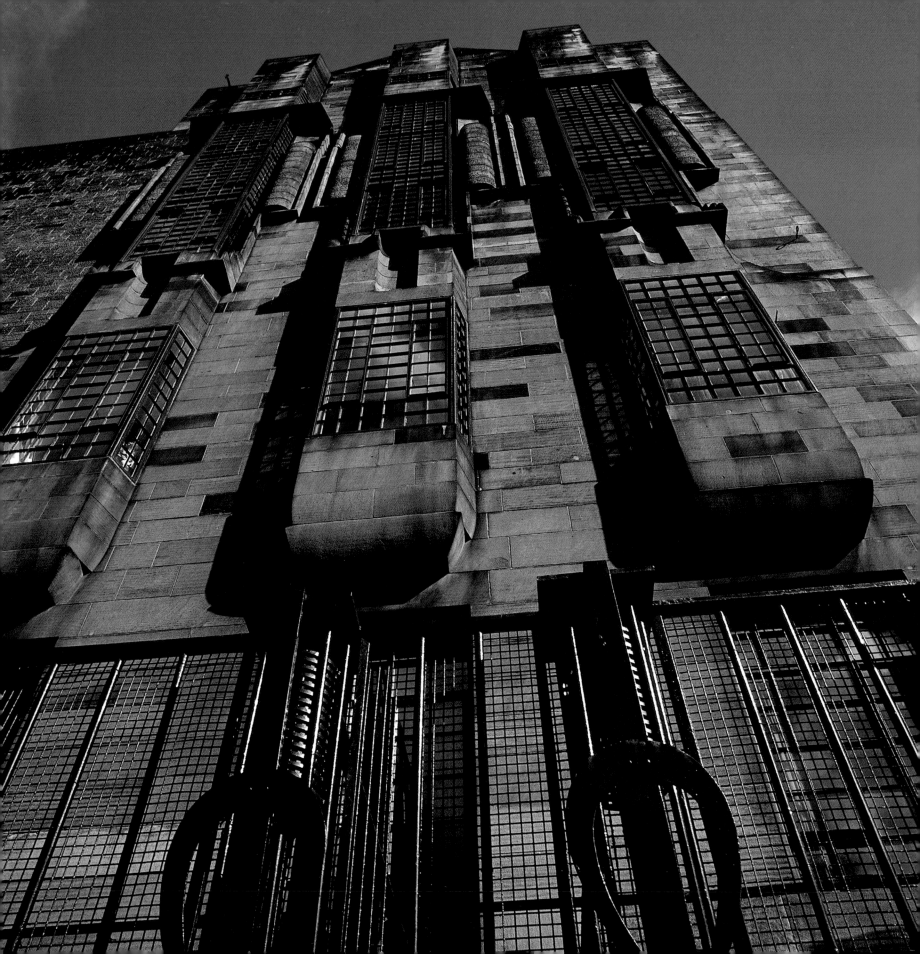

The resulting brief, issued in June 1896, was both specific and ambitious. The site, on Renfrew Street, was also an awkward one, long and narrow, with a steep fall of about 30 feet from north to south. After some weeks of consideration, the twelve competing architects advised the Governors that the task was impossible: the meagre funds allocated to the scheme would not cover the cost of meeting all the requirements of the brief. A lengthy wrangle ensued, and it was eventually decided that the competitors should indicate the proportion of their plans which could be built for the specified amount, the remaining proportion of the building to be completed at a later date once sufficient funds had been raised. The deadline for entries was extended by a month to October; in December, it was announced that a design had been chosen. The winners were Honeyman and Keppie.

The architect of the scheme was, of course, Charles Rennie Mackintosh. Although entries to the competition were anonymous, an approach as distinctive as Mackintosh's would not have been hard to identify, and it must be assumed that Newbery played a significant role in Mackintosh's selection. Even so, all the competition drawings had previously been submitted unattributed for approval to the South Kensington Museum and the Science Museum, whose directors had reached the same conclusion as the competition judges. In Glasgow, once the winner was announced and the drawings were put on display, it was widely believed that Newbery had exerted undue pressure to ensure the success of his brilliant ex-student, but there is no suggestion of this in the surviving records of the competition.

Predictably, the controversy surrounding the publication of the winning design focused on its radical disregard for the traditions of classical or Gothic building. Only Newbery, it was assumed, could have pushed through such a daring proposal with its overtones of Art Nouveau. In specifying a 'plain' building, the Governors were undoubtedly attempting to keep costs within the severely restricted budget, but a utilitarian or functional approach was also the accepted convention for schools and educational institutions, buildings of relatively low prestige. Only the creative vision of a designer such as Mackintosh could transform such plainness into a vehicle for artistry and richness.

Although Mackintosh had been largely responsible for the design of the winning entry, John Keppie was publicly credited as the architect and undertook all official dealings with the client during the first stage. Mackintosh, as an assistant in the firm, was bound by this professional protocol. While the design of the School of Art is eloquent testimony to his creative powers, it is not surprising that in a busy, successful practice such a difficult and unlucrative brief should have been entrusted to a junior.

Three slender shafts, filled with windows, dominate the western end of the School on Dalhousie Street. The upper windows, 25 feet in length, light the Library space. Widely regarded as Mackintosh's finest architectural achievement, the west facade is a clear expression of the interior plan. The dynamic quality is enhanced by the use of small panes which glint and sparkle in the light. The dynamism of the composition is underscored by the recessed windows set in the wall thickness on the adjacent south-facing facade. When the School is approached from the southwest, the vigour of this relationship is strikingly evident.

None of the original competition drawings has survived. Even if they had, they would only have provided an indication of Mackintosh's intentions, not a blueprint for the finished design. Like others who had absorbed the Arts and Crafts notions of artisanship, Mackintosh saw design as a continuing process of refinement and change, part of the activity of construction, not separate from it. This almost organic approach, together with the long period between the initial conception of the building and the completion of its final phase, allowed full scope for Mackintosh's development as a designer; inevitably, it also had serious implications for cost control.

■ ■ ■

Building History

THE FIRST PHASE OF THE SCHOOL OF ART WAS DESIGNED AND BUILT BETWEEN 1897 AND 1899. IT comprised a section running from the east wall to a point just past the entrance. The second phase, built between 1907 and 1909, completed the western half of the building, which included the Library tower with its basement lecture theatre. An attic storey of studios to match the staff studios on top of the western part of the building was added to the eastern side. To achieve this, the original pitched roof was removed and roof lights were installed to correspond with those on the western half. Necessary amendments carried out during the second phase included a new east staircase to improve fire escape provision; and a glazed link to connect the two portions of the building at the upper level.

The foundation stone was laid on 25 May 1898. Inside was a glass container holding a history of the School lettered and illuminated by Jessie King. Little over a year and a half later, on 20 December 1899, the first phase was complete and the building was formally opened. The key, designed by Mackintosh, was officially presented on a cushion made by Margaret Macdonald and Jessie Newbery. Mackintosh remained in the background of the celebrations and did not give a speech.

The following year, the Governors made the unpleasant discovery that the final costs had come in at a third over the original estimate. The extra expenditure was eventually made up four years later, after appeals for further grants. By January 1906, Newbery had again begun to raise money, for the final phase. Over £13,000 ($20,000) was contributed to the fund from a mixture of commercial and

From a dark entrance hall, the eye is led up the main staircase, where light spills down from the toplit Museum above. Here, as in his domestic work, Mackintosh showed extreme sensitivity to the effect of light, contrasting dark enclosed spaces with light, *open areas. Three pairs of tall posts and the treatment of the balusters link the separate levels visually as well as providing a graphic expression of structure. The janitor's box is situated centrally at the foot of the stair.*

■ ■ ■

ENQUIRIES

THE GLASGOW SCHOOL OF ART
NOTICE

ALL VISITORS MUST
REPORT TO THE DESK. NO
ONE IS ALLOWED TO GO
BEYOND THE DESK
WITHOUT PERMISSION.
ANYONE FOUND IN THE
BUILDING WITHOUT THIS
PERMISSION WILL BE
ASKED TO LEAVE.
STUDIOS ARE OFF LIMITS
TO VISITORS.

MUSEUM

Detailing of iron T-girders supporting roof rafters in a basement studio. Here, at the lowest level of the building, each girder end is split and forged into the shape of roots.

private sources. Honeyman, Keppie and Mackintosh gave £100 ($155); Miss Cranston, £20 ($31). To this the Scottish Education Department added an initial sum of £15,000 ($23,250).

Mackintosh, now a partner in his firm, was publicly acknowledged as the architect of this second phase. He resisted early attempts by the Building Committee to make him commit himself to a design for the elevation until he had fully devised the internal plan. The scheme was finally approved in August 1907.

The Governors endeavoured to keep the second phase under tighter financial control, specifying that written approval was required for any alterations to the agreed scheme. Early in 1908 they were predictably furious to discover that the entrance on the west façade had been carried out in 'an extravagant manner' which deviated from the original plans. Monthly progress reports were insisted upon, and further attempts were made to cut costs, which Mackintosh stubbornly resisted. In December 1909, the opening of the finished building was celebrated over the course of several days.

The 'daily fight over three years' which Mackintosh experienced during the first phase of building was matched by the need to justify every single expense during the second. Revisions and reworkings accounted for much of this, of course, and it was not only the Governors who had to be persuaded and cajoled. On at least two occasions craftsmen went on unofficial strike in the face of yet another exacting demand. The architect's insistence on the ends of the iron T-girders which supported the roof rafters in a basement studio each being split and forged in a different intricately fashioned knot caused the blacksmiths to revolt; while the ogee-shaped corridor light wells exasperated the plasterers so much that they too called a halt on the work.

The School of Art: Exterior

The entrance on the west facade of the School (LEFT), framed in stepped mouldings and curved bands of stone, anticipates Art Deco. The governors were furious to discover that Mackintosh had ignored their pleas for economy and treated the doorway in such an 'extravagant manner'.

THE SCHOOL OF ART IS A BUILDING WHICH HAS BEEN DESIGNED FROM THE INSIDE OUT: THAT IS TO SAY, the internal layout of accommodation, from studios to cloakrooms, defines the character of the entire building. The nature of each of these interior spaces is clearly visible on the external face of the building, variations of use and scale signalled by windows of different sizes and shapes and underscored by decorative detail. The emphasis on the practical requirements of the plan is basic to modern architectural design; in Mackintosh's day, it was still a radical idea. The School of Art is transparently honest and truthful in these terms, almost obsessively so.

The basic plan of the building is in the form of an E, with studios arranged the length of the long north frontage on Renfrew Street and the projecting south-facing arms of the E housing various other offices, including lecture rooms and the Library. The entrance, on the north façade, is in the centre of what is basically a logical, nearly symmetrical plan.

:THE:
GLAS-
:G⦿W
SCH8L
⦿F ART

Newbery had specified extremely spacious studios. To provide the even levels of north light essential for painting, correspondingly large windows were required. The grid of transoms and mullions that comprise these massive openings dominates the north façade.

The remarkable and dynamic feature of the front elevation is its asymmetry. The studio windows vary slightly in size, according to the scale of the spaces they light. While the entrance is placed at the physical centre of the building, its treatment subverts this position, justified again by the internal arrangement. There are four bays of windows to the west of the entrance and three bays to the east. The asymmetry is heightened by the symmetrical character of the front railings, which flank the entrance and call attention to its central position. Above the entrance is the Director's office, whose importance is identified by a balcony. The turret form encloses a stair leading from this office to the Director's studio. The attic storey comprises studios, those to the west for members of staff.

The massive east façade of the building on Scott Street, rising to over 80 feet, is dominated by an expanse of unbroken masonry to the north end. To the south, there is an asymmetric arrangement of small windows lighting the janitor's house and a pair of narrow windows signalling the Board Room. The octagonal 'tower' over the side entrance and robust handling of the construction suggests a vital reworking of vernacular forms. The bay 'tower' window rests on one huge stone corbel, an expressive device used to convey the stability of the structure and anchor the asymmetry of the arrangement.

The west façade on Dalhousie Street, entirely redesigned after 1906, represents one of Mackintosh's most consummate architectural compositions. Dominated by the three bays of the Library, slender shafts sweeping upwards into which the long Library windows, 25 feet high, are inserted, this striking elevational treatment is again a direct expression of the plan. The cylindrical drums which flank the Library windows were originally intended to be carved with figures; three of the subjects suggested were Cellini, St Francis and Palladio. The west entrance, which caused the Governors such consternation, is framed in stepped mouldings and curved bands of stone that produce a dynamic sense of movement.

On the south façade, the back of the building, the 'harled' or roughcast finish helps to unify the disparate elements of the three projecting wings, and the symmetrical placing of the windows also lends consistency. On the south-facing façade of the western tower, windows are set back into the thickness of the wall, the recession making a powerful and rhythmic contrast to the projecting Library windows on the adjoining façade.

When the attic storey of studios was added during the second phase, the existing Director's studio prevented access at this level from one side of the building to the other. Mackintosh's solution was to construct a glass-walled passage over the top of the Museum roof in the central wing: the so-called 'hen-run'. A similar adaptation can be seen in Mackintosh's response to the problem created by the need to introduce an additional staircase on the east side as a fire escape. The new stair ran across the pair of west-facing windows lighting the first-floor Board Room; rather than remove the windows, Mackintosh left them in place, fitted them with obscured glass and ran the stair around them.

At the back of the School, the walls (ABOVE) are roughcast, a tough, weather-proof finish typical of Scottish ver-nacular buildings and a treatment well suited to the exposed south facade.

One of the necessary adaptations Mackintosh made during the building of the second phase was the addition of this glazed corridor (RIGHT), nicknamed the 'hen-run', which provides access at the upper level from one side of the building to the other, and runs behind the top of the Director's studio.

Craftsman at work on the wrought-iron window brackets (ABOVE), *c. 1898. Mackintosh typically revised and adapted buildings during the course of their construction, which inevitably cost time, money and good will. This working method, however, reflected his belief that design should not be set apart from the process of making.*

Metalwork provided Mackintosh with an ideal medium for his decorative imagery. The front railings along the length of the north facade (LEFT) are punctuated by eight 'totems', which rise up from clusters of leaves. The metal circles feature cryptic designs, among which can be identified the forms of a bee, scarab and bird. These devices clearly express Mackintosh's deepest spiritual beliefs regarding the essential unity of art and nature; their precise meaning has provided interpreters of Mackintosh's work with a tantalizing subject of study.

'Every portal must have its guardians' wrote Lethaby. The carved roundel over the entrance to the School of Art (RIGHT) features two facing female figures, each holding a rosebud.

The east, north and west façades of the School are made of a hard local sandstone known as Giffnock, and it is Mackintosh's handling of this robust material which gives a thematic unity to the entire building despite its very different elevational treatments. His iconographical use of another material much identified with Glasgow, wrought iron, enriches the front elevation.

Metalwork provided Mackintosh with the opportunity to translate graphic imagery in a direct, almost literal way; characteristically, however decorative the result, functional logic always lies behind it. The best example can be seen in the projecting iron brackets bracing the studio windows – as Macleod has noted, 'the most discussed window brackets in history'. Their humble purpose was to support window cleaners' planks; their intricately wrought finials, graphic abstractions of buds and seedheads, evoke the notion of growth, an appropriate symbol for an educational institution. Pierced metal circles on top of stalks emerging from clusters of leaves, rise above the railings along the north façade. Depicting insect, bird and plant forms, the origin of these symbols has been traced to the form of Japanese family crests, or *Mon*, although their precise meaning is unclear. Etched against the skyline above the School are two iron finials in the form of trees with birds perched on top, a version of the city's coat of arms.

The entrance to the School is marked by a carved roundel in which two facing female figures, each clasping a rosebud, guard the way in. Mackintosh modelled the maquette for the relief carving himself.

The School of Art: Interior

INSIDE THE SCHOOL, A NARROW, ENCLOSED ENTRANCE LEADS TO A DARK VAULTED HALL FROM WHICH rises the central stair, a light-filled well leading up to the first-floor Museum. Both staircase and Museum display Mackintosh's fascination with timber structure, with influences derived from medieval and Japanese constructional methods. The great roof trusses of the top-lit Museum have king posts incised with hearts; this motif, the flat-capped newel posts and extended balusters recall the work of Voysey. Projecting over the stairwell on the half landing is another version of Glasgow's coat of arms, featuring the bird, tree, fish and bell emblems of its patron saint, Mungo.

Just as the dark entrance leads the eye on to the light of the staircase, a dark ante-room on the first floor provides a dramatic foil for the pristine decoration of the Director's office, one of Mackintosh's first white interiors. White-painted panelling is taken up two-thirds of the wall, linking, in typical Mackintosh fashion, the tops of doors, cupboards and fireplace surround. The ceiling drops down to form an alcove by the arched window, defining a study area and elegantly fusing exterior and interior.

Another white interior is the original Board Room, now the Mackintosh Room. The pairs of tall bay windows at either end of the room create an airy, light-filled space; two steel beams, painted white, span the ceiling.

The vast studios on the north side of the building extend to a height of 17 feet on the ground level, 26 feet on the first-floor level. Equipped with Mackintosh-designed easels and a system of electrical lights on pulleys, the studios were heated by hot air ducted through wall grilles. This ingeniously integrated system, which contributed much to the practical efficiency of the School, may have exploited, as has been suggested, heating technology first developed in the context of ship-fitting. Electric studio clocks, designed by Mackintosh, synchronized centrally, ensured accurate timekeeping.

A first-floor corridor on the east side was originally used as a place to display the School's collection of plaster casts. The corridor is top lit by ogee-shaped light wells, the same feature which caused such uproar among the craftsmen working on the construction of the School. Basement studios, for activities which required less daylight such as ceramics, metalwork and woodcarving, are lit by area skylights. The lecture theatre is also at this level, as well as two top-lit studios inserted between the arms of the E-shaped plan.

During the second phase, the ground-floor studio immediately to the east of the entrance was converted into a series of rooms, one of which was a new Board Room; owing to pressure on space, the original Board Room had been co-opted as an additional studio. This formal dark-panelled room

The Director's Office, 1897–99, was one of Mackintosh's first white interiors. With the recent addition of the light fittings and desk, the room has finally been completed to Mackintosh's original specification. White painted panelling, taken up to two-thirds of the wall height, aligns with the top of doors and fire surround and drops down in a graceful curve to meet the arched window. A staircase leads from this room to the Director's private studio above. As the stair is too narrow for large paintings to be moved out of the studio, a slit was cut in the studio floor to allow canvases to be lowered to the level below.

**:THE:
GLAS-
:G°W
SCH8L
°F ART**

contains the only classical reference in the School, eight carved pilasters headed with egg-and-dart moulding: in Mackintosh's adaptation, the natural origins of this classical motif surge into view. The idiosyncratic pattern of squares and rectangles randomly arranged on the fluting of the pilasters (each of which is different from the others) has been compared by some to musical notation: Mackintosh himself made the link between musical and architectural composition in his lecture on 'Seemliness'. Dr Howarth suggests that these classical references might have been Mackintosh's sarcastic way of cocking a snook at the members of the architectural establishment who sat on the Board of Governors.

Throughout the School, such 'musical' variations on a theme can be seen in various decorative devices. White, blue and green tiles set in a square in various permutations serve as directional indicators on the stairs; doors are enriched with stained-glass symbols of insects, flowers and seedheads; squares feature again cut into chair-backs, as a motif on clock faces, pierced in metal light fittings.

For much of the School's interior, the emphasis is on rugged utility of finish – exposed steel and timber beams, exposed brickwork, plain rendering – creating a highly robust and defiantly 'plain' working environment. The exception is the Library, identified by most commentators as Mackintosh's finest interior: 'the masterpiece within the masterwork'.

The intensity of feeling aroused by this room marks it as one of the great architectural spaces of any age. At once complex and self-explanatory, rich and unadorned, it embodies the ever-present tension between the decorative and the structural in Mackintosh's work, and represents its finest resolution.

The Library consists of three layers: the Library itself, its gallery and a concealed book store on the level above, now used as an exhibition area. The complexities of the Library's construction arise from the deliberate illusion that the posts which run from floor to ceiling in the main space act as a support for its roof. In fact, what is perceived as the roof of the Library is the floor of the store-room above it; this floor is actually suspended from metal hangers dropped down from the great cast-iron beams which cross the store-room ceiling, which itself marks the full extent of the Library space.

There are perfectly sound reasons for this structural complexity. The three levels of the Library space occupy one complete first-floor studio height. If the store-room floor with its heavy burden of books had not been

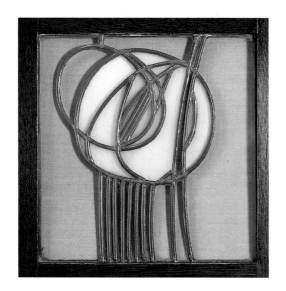

Stained glass panels featuring rosebuds, seeds, insect and bird forms mark entrance ways throughout the School.

One of Mackintosh's brilliantly idiosyncratic and innovative light fittings, on display in The Mackintosh Room at the School of Art. Originally designed for Windyhill in 1901, where it hung over the staircase, this fitting was part of the Davidson bequest.

The original Board Room (RIGHT), now The Mackintosh Room, contains furniture and light fittings from Windyhill and a reproduction of the carpet designed for The Hill House. Another white interior, filled with natural light from pairs of tall curved windows at either end, the Board Room apparently found little favour with the governors of the School and was co-opted as additional studio space before the second phase of the building was completed.

suspended from above, substantial supports would have been needed below, which would have ruled out the delicate construction of the Library interior. As the Library windows extend the entire height of the space, it is possible to look up in the bays beyond the gallery to glimpse internal windows to the hidden store-room above, thus appreciating the structural sleight-of-hand.

The Library is, as it has been described, a 'timber cage' suspended within the masonry and steel construction of the building, a structural system which elsewhere provides the clear views essential in the studios and lecture theatre. In the Library, the positioning of the oak posts, which defines the layout of the room, marks the location of the great steel beams on which they rest. The relative fineness of these apparent timber supports as they rise up to the Library ceiling heightens the sense of structural drama.

The timber components are handled like a construction kit. The gallery, which runs along all four sides of the Library, rests on pairs of beams projected out from the walls to clasp the posts. Beneath these pegged joints, the posts are strengthened with wooden facing, as if the projecting beams had turned through a right-angle. The posts, which support the gallery, have to rest on the main floor beams; in the original 1897 design, the gallery was taken out the full width to meet them. Mackintosh's brilliant later revision was to narrow the gallery to increase the central area. Decorative uprights fill the resulting gaps between posts and gallery and are enriched with rippling multi-coloured scalloped or 'waggon-chamfered' edges. Curved wooden panels on the front of the gallery extend below in oddly carved and pierced sections.

The Library is Mackintosh's supreme achievement, a rhythmical composition in timber which powerfully evokes the spirit of growth. The delicacy of the Library interior underscores the sense of drama and mystery. Small touches of primary colour on the waggon-chamfered edges of the balusters which fill the gaps between the upright posts and gallery suggest the effect of dappled light.

The impression created by the rhythm of these posts and wooden elements, the light filtering down from the tall windows, and the central pool of illumination from thirteen lamps suspended low over the desks, has been compared to a grove of trees, a comparison which would have been enhanced by the fine spindle-backs of the original library chairs (of which only six remain). It may well be that the tree of knowledge, with its spreading roots and branches of learning, is evoked here in three-dimensional form; the tree was always a potent symbol for Mackintosh. Ripening, fruition – the spirit of growth imbues the decorative detail of the entire School.

The Library provides strong evidence for those who claim Mackintosh as the forerunner of modernism. Along with the School as a whole, it has become a place of architectural pilgrimage, the subject of intense study. Yet the School does not, as is sometimes claimed, emerge unheralded by any historic or contemporary antecedent. Scholarly detection has identified many strands of influence that might have shaped Mackintosh's ideas as he was designing and constructing the School, references that include the work of contemporaries such as Norman Shaw, Voysey, Mackmurdo and Lethaby,

Clustered over the central table is a group of remarkable light fittings which direct light downwards. Grouping fittings made practical sense at a time when wattage was low, but the central pool of light has an equally poetic purpose.

as well as more ancient sources such as traditional Japanese construction, great Elizabethan houses such as Montacute and various features of Scottish castles.

What is truly great about the School of Art is Mackintosh's ability to meld these concepts and ideas into a fully integrated work of his own imagination. The mysterious poetry of its synthetic blend of decoration and construction is unique and original: it is, above all, a work of art in which art can be made.

When the School was finally complete, contemporary opinion was predictably divided. The first phase was variously castigated as resembling a 'poorhouse' or 'house of correction' and lauded as a 'monument to the strong originality and artistic conception of the Glasgow designers'; at the official handover of the second phase, Sir John Stirling Maxwell perceptively praised Mackintosh for showing 'that it was possible to have a good building without plastering it over with the traditional, expensive and often ugly ornament'. The Governors declared that they were 'not aware of any city that possesses a more complete edifice devoted to Art Education, nor one better adapted to its purpose'. The rest was silence, a deep critical apathy that lasted many years.

Today, nearly a century later after it was first conceived, the School is still in use, serving the purpose for which it was designed and serving it well.

Windyhill

Kilmacolm, Renfrewshire
Client: William Davidson junior
Built: 1900–01

WINDYHILL WAS MACKINTOSH'S FIRST SIGNIFICANT INDEPENDENT COMMISSION, DESIGNED AT A TIME of intense interest in British domestic building; it was also Mackintosh's first opportunity to design both architecture and furniture in a domestic context. The work came his way through his connection with the Davidson family. William Davidson senior was a prominent Glasgow businessman and patron of the arts, who had a special interest in the work of the Glasgow Boys. It is thought that Mackintosh was first introduced to the family by Francis Newbery; between 1894 and 1897 he designed some pieces of furniture for their home, Gladsmuir, which the elder Davidsons shared with their son, William Davidson junior, and his family. The Davidsons became ardent admirers of the work of the young architect.

'Windyhill', Kilmacolm, 1901, from the northwest. 'Windyhill', commissioned by the Davidsons, was Mackintosh's first opportunity to design a family house. The stylized form of the trees and shrubs, which feature in Mackintosh's perspective drawings, recall the sparse Japanese-style arrangements of twigs and branches that appear in his room settings and interiors.

Windyhill, commissioned by the younger William Davidson as a family home, occupies a steep site at the summit of a hill, with wide open views of the surrounding countryside. No records of the early stages of the project survive, but it is reasonable to assume that Mackintosh, in his usual fashion, took care first to devise the plan before going on to consider the elevations.

The simple plan of this family house is traditionally arranged in an L-shape, with the shorter arm of the L on the ground floor comprising a service wing of kitchen, laundry and utility rooms, and the longer arm taken up with dining-room, living-room, playroom and a 'lounge-hall' leading to a staircase set in a semicircular bay. The hall apparently served as a dining-room for large parties. There are seven bedrooms on the second floor. The internal arrangement is proof of Mackintosh's sensitivity to the practicalities of domestic life.

From the exterior, Windyhill reveals Mackintosh's modern reworking of traditional features. The masonry structure of the house is finished in grey roughcast or 'harling', a means of weatherproofing Scottish houses that had been in use since the fifteenth century. The roughcasting is taken right up against the window frames in a practical but severe fashion. The pitched roofs, gable ends and stout chimneys are other obvious vernacular elements. Small windows in a somewhat restless variety of shapes and sizes punctuate the plain façades. The tall narrow windows lighting the staircase prefigure a common feature of domestic architecture twenty years later.

The house is approached from the north. Within the sheltering angle of the L, a square pool set in a square courtyard in front of the entrance introduces a familiar theme, later taken up in the design of a large semicircular garden seat incorporated at the bottom of the garden and originally intended to be placed facing the house. At the rear of the house, on the south side, the elevation is stark and severe; shutters were later added by the Davidsons to mitigate its bleak appearance, although they did not seem much troubled by local opinion which compared the house to a barracks.

In later years, the house was altered internally, but some restoration has since been carried out. In the original scheme, the lounge-hall leading to the main stair was papered in white, graphically outlined with dark oak strips. The broad panelled stair rose up from one end of the hall; there was no handrail, and the balustrading was simply constructed of flat boards infilled with coloured glass squares. The drawing-room was plain from floor to ceiling, with dark papering on one west wall, while the dining-room was panelled in dark-stained wood up to picture-rail height. The main bedroom was white, with delicate touches of green and mauve.

Mackintosh designed some, but not all, of the furniture and fittings for the house, concentrating his efforts on the drawing-room, playroom, hall and master bedroom. Davidson apparently also brought the Gladsmuir furniture with him to Windyhill. The white drawing-room fireplace, which featured a gold mosaic surround into which were set five rose motifs in coloured glass and enamel, was particularly fine and original. The striking gas light fittings in the hall were open lanterns composed of square glass panes. Later designs created for Windyhill included a pyramidal dovecote and a square-gridded trellis arbour for the garden.

In 1920, William Davidson bought the Mackintoshes' former home, 78 Southpark Avenue, together with some of its furniture. He remained a loyal admirer of Mackintosh's work and played an important role in preserving what remained of the architect's drawings and paintings after his death. It was in the basement of his Glasgow firm that the collection was later researched by Dr Howarth, Mackintosh's biographer. After Davidson's death, his sons Hamish and Cameron were instrumental in the process by which 78 Southpark Avenue was acquired by the University of Glasgow; they donated the contents in memory of their father along with many of the Windyhill pieces, most notably the master bed, to the Glasgow School of Art.

Mackintosh's association with the Davidsons was long and affectionate. Hamish Davidson recalled many Christmas gifts from 'Uncle Tosh'; on one occasion Mackintosh, playing the role of Father Christmas, set his robes alight on the Christmas tree candles and had to be doused in the square courtyard pool. Like The Hill House, Windyhill demonstrates what Mackintosh was able to achieve in the right circumstances and for the right clients. His friendship with the Davidsons gave him the insight he believed important for any architect commissioned to design a family home; their enthusiasm was vital for the full expression of his architectural ideas.

The hall and staircase at Windyhill. Only a few rooms at Windyhill were furnished by Mackintosh, among them the hall, which functioned as a dining room for large family gatherings. The hall furniture includes a long table, with an accompanying square table which could be used as an extension, a pair of benches and chairs with high tapering backs, all in a simple robust style.

The Hill House

Helensburgh, Dunbartonshire
Built: 1902–04
Client: W. W. Blackie

■ ■ ■

THE HILL HOUSE IS MACKINTOSH'S FINEST AND LARGEST DOMESTIC SCHEME. RECENTLY RESTORED, IT IS now owned by the National Trust for Scotland.

Mackintosh's client for this project, Walter Blackie, was a prosperous Glaswegian publisher who had acquired a site in Helensburgh, where he intended to build a house for his young family. A new railway connection had brought Helensburgh within commuting distance of Glasgow, and the gently sloping hillside site that Blackie had purchased offered sweeping views of the Firth of Clyde.

Although Blackie had never met Mackintosh, he was much taken with the design of the Glasgow School of Art, of which the first stage of construction had been completed in 1899. It was on the recommendation of Talwin Morris, Art Director at Blackie and Son, that Walter Blackie eventually approached Mackintosh to design a villa for his own site – although at first he was sceptical about whether the architect of such an imposing civic building would accept a small domestic commission. At their first meeting, Blackie was astonished to discover how young Mackintosh was.

The brief that Blackie gave Mackintosh was, by his own admission, chiefly negative. But by a fortunate conjunction, his taste and views coincided perfectly with those of his chosen architect. Blackie was keen to avoid the characteristic Victorian heaviness of design and ornamentation and favoured a building that would impress the onlooker through its sheer presence rather than one which existed solely as an excuse for intricate stylistic detail. He felt instinctively that slate roofs and grey roughcast walls would harmonize better with the Scottish climate and landscape than red roof tiles, brick, timber and render.

After their initial meeting, there followed a period of getting to know one another. Mackintosh took the Blackies to Windyhill, where they could see

The Hill House, Helensburgh, viewed from the rear. A circular staircase tower is placed in the angle between the two rambling wings of the building, a reference to Scottish vernacular architecture. To the west are the main family living quarters, while the east wing houses service rooms.

The window of the main bedroom is flanked by 'shutters' sculpted in concrete, which echo the movable shutters fitted in the interior of the room.

■ ■ ■

many of his architectural ideas in practice. He visited them at home at Dunblane to get acquainted with the needs and activities of the family. On his visit to the Blackie home, Mackintosh spotted a small wardrobe in the hall, a design he had produced in earlier days for Guthrie and Wells and which the Blackies had bought knowing nothing of its designer. Both sides took this as an omen that the collaboration would prove fruitful.

The first stage in the design of The Hill House consisted of working up plans and internal layouts. An unexpected pregnancy in the Blackie family led to a few design alterations to accommodate a nursery for the new baby. With Mackintosh, Blackie later recalled, 'the practical purpose came first. The pleasing design followed of itself . . .'

The plan resembles that of Windyhill, broadly L-shaped, with the principal rooms laid out in a similar way, although the house is entered from the west end, with a small dark vestibule giving on to a larger main hall used as a reception area. There is an additional attic storey over the service wing. It is amusing to note that Mackintosh thoughtfully placed the nursery for the new baby at the opposite end of the house from the library; the site of this room, immediately off the small entrance hall, allowed Blackie's business meetings to take place without disrupting the household or being disrupted by it.

When the plans and layouts were approved, Mackintosh turned his attention to the external elevations. Wrought-iron gates, whose design hints at what is to come, lead to the entrance at the west end of the house. At the rear, the asymmetrical form of the house is punctuated by a tower placed in the angle between the two rambling wings, a feature which recalls traditional Scottish building. As at Windyhill, the windows vary in size and shape, but their distribution, although irregular, has a more balanced effect. The walls are finished in roughcast rendering and the roof is dark blue-grey slate. The precise colour of roof slate that Mackintosh wanted was only available from one particular quarry, Ballachulish, which was immobilized by a strike at a critical point in the construction of the house. Rather than choose another colour, Mackintosh insisted on waiting until the quarry resumed production.

Interior spaces follow the characteristic Mackintosh sequence and display his acute sensitivity to the play of natural light. From the hall, with its exposed woodwork, strong rectilinearity and glints of colour, the eye is led up the light-filled stairwell, the rhythmic verticals of the balusters and extended newel post rising up to the next level.

The drawing-room incorporates a light-filled bay fitted with a window seat and doors giving out on to the garden; another recess, at right angles to it, is designed to accommodate a piano or serve as a

The 'summer end' of the drawing room (OVERLEAF) *comprises a light-filled bay fitted with a window seat overlooking the garden. The table designed for this location in 1908 is a masterful composition of intersecting squares. As the sun moves across the sky, the shadows cast by the table shift and change, infusing the inanimate with a dynamic, living quality.*

The entrance hall at The Hill House is a rich and complex space, aligned with the main axis of the house. Blackie's study is adjacent to the main door, providing direct access for business callers. The stair rises from the main part of the hall, the open *balustrading permitting a visual connection between levels. The stencilled frieze on the panels is an abstract design synthesizing geometric and organic motifs in an evocative summary of Mackintosh's approach.*

:THE:
:HILL:
HOUSE

▪THE▪
▪HILL▪
H◌USE

The drawing room wall sconces feature stained glass panels which echo the stencilled rose and trellis design on the wall. Mackintosh originally lit the room with four pendant fittings, which were later removed at the request of Mrs Blackie. At this point, the ceiling was repainted a darker colour, probably a dull warm red.

stage for family theatricals. The south-facing bay forms a 'summer focus', while the other end of the room, enclosed and more inward-looking for winter evenings, is dominated by the fireplace with its overmantel gesso panel by Margaret Macdonald. The high-backed couch which Mackintosh designed for this room was placed so that its occupants were shielded from penetrating winter draughts. The walls are white, delicately stencilled in grey, rose and green; the picture rail is aligned with the height of the two recesses, serving to draw together the various areas within a room so hospitably arranged for family activities.

In the original decoration, the frieze and ceiling in the drawing-room were both painted white, and large light fittings hung from the ceiling, aligned with the picture rail. Mrs Blackie asked Mackintosh to remove these at a later date, probably around 1912 when he was engaged in some decorative repairs and improvements. When the lights were taken down, the balance of the room was affected and Mackintosh painted the ceiling to reduce its impact. The precise colour, variously described as 'plum'

Details taken from the white painted washstand in the main bedroom show a fusion of organic and geometric motifs. In later pieces, organic references were almost entirely abandoned in favour of the square.

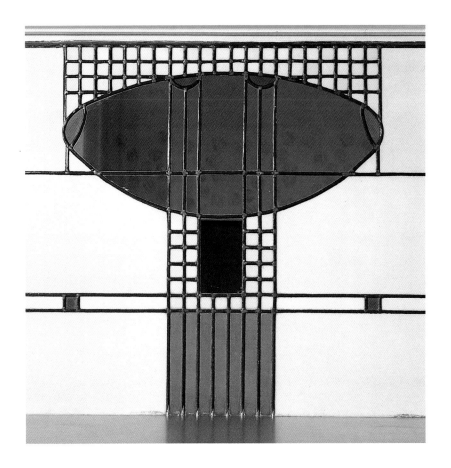

in Mackintosh's notes, or black washed with buttermilk in the recollection of the Blackie daughters, is not known, although it is likely that the flat black of the ceiling in a later restoration, a colour which tends to dominate the drawing-room, must be mistaken.

The library is more soberly treated, with horizontal bands of dark oak shelves and cupboards fitted around its perimeter. The dining-room is also panelled in dark-stained pine; Mackintosh believed that dark walls helped to concentrate the attention where it belonged – on the dining-table with its gleam of silverware, glass and candlelight.

By contrast, the intimacy of the main bedroom is expressed in its soft, smooth white decoration and furnishings. The bed is set in a recess defined by a vaulted ceiling and echoed in the form of the shallow curved wall adjacent to it, while built-in corner seating, wardrobes, a mirror and furniture placement further distinguish between the sleeping area and that part intended to function as a dressing area and morning room. With its tonal purity and precision of detail this room remains one of Mackintosh's most evocative interiors.

Fireplaces and fire tongs, fitted cupboards, chairs and tables, stencilled wall designs and light fittings – there is scarcely an aspect of interior fitting and furnishing to which Mackintosh did not devote the utmost care and attention. Many of his ideas began with practical considerations. A napery cupboard, for example, intricately fitted with trays and drawers to the housekeeper's specification, is heated by a hot-water cylinder, built into the wall behind, to keep the linen warm and dry. The drawing-room window seat incorporates magazine racks at either end and a radiator underneath, while a panelled inglenook on an upper landing provides just the sort of delightful gathering place most appealing to children. The light fittings, initially designed for gas, proved to adapt readily to electrification. In anticipating every need, Mackintosh created a home which truly reflected his client's way of life.

Mackintosh's intense attention to detail could be carried to extremes. He apparently insisted that the trees on the site be clipped to a shape which matched those on his architectural drawings, and the Blackie children later recalled the architect berating Mrs Blackie for a flower arrangement which clashed with the colour scheme in the hall. The Blackies could hardly have objected to the cost; unusually for a Mackintosh project, the final account came in well under the original estimate. However, Blackie could not afford to commission new furniture for the entire house; the hall and master bedroom are the only rooms in which every piece has been designed by the architect.

Many accounts of The Hill House barely mention the name of Margaret Macdonald, but it must be noted that she worked alongside Mackintosh in the creation of these much admired rooms. It was Margaret, for example, who made the shimmering gesso panel installed above the drawing-room

The main bedroom comprises a sleeping area, sheltering under its curved ceiling, and a dressing area-cum-morning room. The shallow curve of the ceiling vault is completed by the carved curve at the foot of the bed. Each drawer in the small jewellery cabinet beneath the window has a different lock and key. The cheval mirror, positioned between two sash windows, has pedestals pierced with a grid of squares. Recent restoration work has reinstated the delicate wall stencilling of roseheads and trellis which appears in Mackintosh's original design and was subsequently painted over.

fireplace, and it is her embroidery which delicately embellishes curtains and lampshades. If The Hill House is Mackintosh's finest achievement in the realm of domestic building, it is also among the most accomplished works of their creative partnership, powerful evidence of a shared sensibility.

In the detailing of The Hill House, the thematic play of the square is ever-present. The porch at the entrance is decorated with a stencilled pattern that, almost more than any other motif, encapsulates Mackintosh's unique vision. Over a mesh of squares drifts the whited-out silhouette of a plant form, a stem topped by flower or seedhead: nature and order, decoration and structure in perfect harmony; a signature for a work whose every detail speaks of its creator.

In 1904 the Blackies finally took up residence. Mackintosh handed over the house with the following words:

Here is the house. It is not an Italian villa, an English mansion house, a Swiss chalet or a Scotch castle. It is a dwelling house.

Mackintosh Interiors

120 Mains Street, 1900
78 Southpark Avenue, 1906
Reconstructed as
The Mackintosh House, Hunterian Art Gallery, University of Glasgow, 1981

WITH NO CLIENTS TO PLEASE, AND NO OFFICIAL AUTHORITIES TO PLACATE, THE INTERIORS Mackintosh created with his wife Margaret for their own use present particularly complete examples of his visionary ideas in practice. In many cases, aspects of design later explored in other contexts found their first expression in these rooms; their all-embracing unity distils the essence of his approach.

MACK-INTOSH INTER-IORS

The beautiful hall clock at The Hill House dates from 1904, and is made of dark stained pine, with a painted metal face and brass hands and weights. The chair, one of four created for the hall, is unstained oak. The sturdy design features an angled lattice back, echoing the square cutouts on the hall table. The carpet designed for the hall also features groups of squares arranged around its perimeter. The upper hall is furnished to serve as a reception room.

The flat at 120 Mains Street (later Blythswood Street) was decorated and furnished in anticipation of the Mackintoshes' marriage in August 1900. Mackintosh and his wife remained here until 1906, at which time Mackintosh bought a house in Hillhead, a fashionable district of Glasgow near the University. Many of the original furnishings and fittings designed for Mains Street were reinstalled at 78 Southpark Avenue (originally 6 Florentine Terrace) and, with few exceptions, the two homes shared the same basic decorative formula.

After Mackintosh left Glasgow in 1914, the Southpark Avenue house remained empty until it was sold, complete with most of its contents, to William Davidson in 1920. The interiors and furnishings survived in a remarkably intact state up until Davidson's death in 1945, when they were acquired by the University of Glasgow. The deteriorating structural condition of the house, coupled with the University's plans for expansion in the immediate neighbourhood, eventually led to a plan to reconstruct the original Mackintosh interiors within the framework of a new building. In 1981 The Mackintosh House, part of the Hunterian Art Gallery, was officially opened; here furniture and fittings from the dismantled Southpark Avenue interiors, held in storage for the previous decades following the demolition of the house, are displayed in a careful reconstruction of the original rooms.

The Mains Street flat, at which Mackintosh was able to carry out no structural alterations, is the core work. In this conversion of a typical Glaswegian tenement, Mackintosh subtly altered the interior proportions to provide a sympathetic framework for his decorative and design ideas. The four principal apartments comprised the drawing-room and studio, the dining-room and the master bedroom.

The drawing-room, which, together with the Director's room at the School of Art, is among the first of Mackintosh's white interiors, was sparsely arranged, in striking contrast to the characteristically overblown and heavy decoration of the Edwardian period. Mackintosh employed a number of strategies to adjust the existing proportions of this nineteenth-century room, with its elaborate detailing and high ceilings. He removed the central ceiling rose (medallion); the cornice (crown molding), skirtings (baseboards), window architraves and door were retained and painted white. A broad white wooden rail ending in a narrow flat shelf was installed at picture-rail height, taken around the perimeter of the room and extended across the windows. Above this line, the frieze and ceiling were painted white; below, narrow wooden strips divided the wall surface into panels covered with pale grey painted canvas. The windows were covered in fine muslin to filter the light and dressed with simple curtains embroidered by Margaret. Artificial lighting was provided by twelve gas jets, in three groups of four, suspended from the ceiling.

The dining-room, by contrast, had dark walls, papered in coarse brown wrapping paper, and a white-painted frieze and ceiling. Tapering wooden posts supported wall-mounted candelabra, and a broad black picture rail was installed to align with the top of the door and the window frames. Both the bedroom and the studio were painted white. The floor was covered in pale grey fitted carpet.

The Mains Street flat was entirely furnished with pieces of Mackintosh's design, many of which were painted white. All the bedroom furniture was white, including the four-poster bed with its

The Mackintosh House (OVERLEAF), part of the Hunterian Gallery, Glasgow, is a reconstruction of interiors from 78 Southpark Avenue, featuring many of the original details and furniture. The studio-drawing room, furnished and decorated almost entirely in a soft, luminous white, displays Mackintosh's manipulation of the conventional proportions of a nineteenth-century interior. The light fittings hang at precisely the level of the flat picture rail, from which the original curtains, embroidered by Margaret, were also suspended.

The fluid curves of the cheval mirror (RIGHT) designed for the bedroom at 120 Mains Street in 1900 suggest the plasticity of a material other than wood. Mackintosh's use of white to hide the grain of timber evokes sensuality and intimacy. This mirror was exhibited in Vienna in 1900.

MACK- INT⚬SH INTER- ▪IORS

embroidered hangings and the double wardrobe, both of which featured delicate inlays of coloured glass. In the drawing-room, a minimal and precise arrangement of chairs and small tables was anchored by a bookcase and desk set against flanking walls. The remaining wall was dominated by a large white fireplace with broad flat curves and shallow square recesses. The studio fireplace was simply panelled in white-painted planks, a treatment which probably concealed an existing mantelpiece.

In 1906 the Mackintoshes moved to Southpark Avenue, taking much of the Mains Street furniture and fittings with them. Their new home was an end-of-terrace stone house built in the 1860s. The front of the house faced east; there were four storeys in all, including an attic, with bay windows on the ground and first floors.

Mackintosh carried out rather more extensive alterations to this house, particularly on the first and second floors. One external change was to narrow the front entrance, remove the porch and replace the door; the new door was white, with inserts of square purple glass.

On the first floor, Mackintosh removed a partition wall to form an L-shaped apartment, a combined drawing-room and studio. The entrance to the room was through the studio end at the rear of the house; the large drawing-room ran the width of the house at the front. He left the bay window and the tall window beside it unaltered, but replaced the window on the adjoining wall (the gable end of the house) with a long, low casement, provided, he said, for his wife, 'so that she can watch the sunsets'.

Two bedrooms on the second floor were similarly combined to make an L-shaped room. On the attic storey, there was a guest bedroom with French windows opening out on to a roof terrace.

The proportional strategies first adopted at Mains Street were again employed at Southpark Avenue. In the drawing-room, a broad flat picture rail ran around the room, aligning with the top of the new opening between drawing-room and studio. The rail was continued across the bay and its flanking window and the upper portion boxed in to reduce their apparent height. Cornice and ceiling rose were removed and the entire apartment was painted white. With muslin at the bay window and warm south light spilling into the room from the new casement, the effect was exceptionally airy and bright. In the studio, the picture rail continued at the same level, with panels of coloured glass inserted where it crossed the tall rear window. Electric lights hung low on a level with the rail.

The white painted desk and chair were originally created for the drawing room at the Mains Street flat in 1900, the year of the Mackintoshes' marriage. The doors, with their silvered panels probably worked by Margaret, open to reveal a fitted interior. Mackintosh took great care to design the interior fittings of desks and wardrobes, to suit the precise requirements of their contents. The remarkable quality of this white interior, which made an indelible impression on those who visited it, reflects Mackintosh's lifelong obsession with light, as the mainspring of life. Windows were hung with unlined muslin to diffuse the light, so that the entire room seemed to radiate an inner glow. The long casement window, just visible to the left of the photograph, was installed by Mackintosh for Margaret, so she could 'watch the sunsets'.

The Mains Street drawing-room fireplace was installed and a new fireplace created for the studio. On the ground floor, the dining-room followed the usual pattern, with dark brown wrapping paper taken up to the low picture rail and stencilled with a design in black, pink, silver and green; the fireplace here also came from Mains Street. It is likely that the hall was papered in a similar fashion.

The bedroom was furnished with the same Mains Street pieces, with the four-poster bed set back in the recess formed by the short arm of the L. The Mains Street fireplace was also installed here. The narrow staircase which led up from this level to the attic bedroom was papered in broad black and white stripes.

The Mackintosh House, where the Southpark Avenue rooms have now been reconstructed, occupies three levels of a building situated one block west of the original site. The rooms share the same orientation; nearly all the internal features, down to the window sashes and balusters, are original.

The radical nature of these rooms, their astonishing simplicity and refinement, created an indelible impression on all those who visited them: 'an oasis, a revelation, a delight', in the words of one admiring contemporary. Several decades before the coining of the famous catch-phrase, Mackintosh's interiors demonstrated incontrovertibly that less could be more. But however minimal the arrangement or restrained the décor, the final effect was never bleakly utilitarian; the delight in light and colour, the orchestration of decorative motifs invested these pure spaces with richness, mystery and meaning.

The entrance to The Mackintosh House reveals the way in which Mackintosh remodelled the original nineteenth-century proportions at 78 Southpark Avenue. He removed the existing porch, and replaced outer storm doors with a new, narrower door. In the hall, panelling is angled to meet the narrowed entrance.

The decoration of the dining room at Southpark Avenue followed the typical Mackintosh formula. Walls were dark and subdued, set off by a plain painted white frieze and ceiling. The coarse brown wallpaper was stencilled with a trellis design ornamented by glinting silver ovals. The effect is to concentrate attention on the table and the ceremony of dining.

Willow Tea Rooms

**217 Sauchiehall Street, Glasgow
Client: Miss Catherine Cranston
Designed and built: 1903**

 THE WILLOW TEA ROOMS BUILDING REPRESENTS THE MOST COMPLETE AND ACCOMPLISHED EXAMPLE OF all the schemes Mackintosh executed for Miss Cranston during a twenty-year association. Recently restored, it now houses a jeweller's and gift shop; the Room de Luxe reopened as a tea room in 1983.

Miss Cranston and the Tea-room Phenomenon

THE EMERGENCE OF THE TEA ROOM IN THE LATE NINETEENTH CENTURY WAS A DEVELOPMENT peculiar to Glasgow. The commercial and industrial expansion of the city brought enormous social change in its wake; a growing working population was drawn to the centre from the rural outskirts. The new business community, with its driving entrepreneurial spirit, sponsored wide-ranging developments in trade and retailing. Department stores, hotels and catering establishments addressed the needs of the leisured middle class.

The tea room filled a particular gap in the market. Drunkenness was an increasing social problem, the inevitable accompaniment of industrial expansion; the temperance movement was correspondingly strong in Scotland. There was an awareness of the need for places where office workers and clerks could take light refreshment in the middle of the day and return to their desks in a sober condition. At the same time, women were venturing out of the home, and the tea rooms provided a genteel environment where they could partake of sweets, cakes, light meals and non-alcoholic drinks unchaperoned. In their later manifestations, such establishments might consist of a whole complex of lunch rooms, tea rooms, smoking, billiard, reading and games rooms catering for the needs of both sexes.

ABOVE: *Catherine Cranston (1849–1934) was an astute businesswoman who established Glasgow as 'a very Tokyo for tea Rooms'. She was a somewhat eccentric figure who retained throughout her life the mid-Victorian dress style of her youth.*

Mackintosh's first commission from Miss Cranston was to execute stencilled mural decorations for her Buchanan Street Tea Rooms (RIGHT). *The stylized female figures enclosed within thickets of roses which featured in the Ladies' Room (1897) call to mind Mackintosh's poster designs of the same period, but are also closely related to* Part Seen Imagined Part, *a watercolour of 1896 which Mackintosh presented to Margaret Macdonald. The Studio praised the murals, commenting that by subtle variations of detail Mackintosh had avoided the mechanical look normally associated with stencilling.*

The first Glasgow tea room was opened in 1875 by Stuart Cranston, a tea dealer and one of a family of hotel-keepers. Cranston's venture proved highly successful, and he went on to build a local empire of similar establishments on the basis of it. But it was his sister and business rival, Kate, who was instrumental in the process which led to the Glasgow tea room becoming a byword for artistic advance and excellence.

Kate Cranston (1849–1934) was a strong-minded businesswoman, with the rare determination to succeed in the male commercial world. She cut a somewhat eccentric figure in turn-of-the-century Glasgow, in her flounced, ruffled and crinolined dresses, the old-fashioned style of her youth which she retained throughout her life. She was a perfectionist, devoted to the highest quality in every aspect of her business, a trait with which Mackintosh undoubtedly sympathized: he allowed Miss Cranston to arrange the flowers in the tea-room interiors, a task which on another occasion he was not even prepared to delegate to his mentor Newbery.

Miss Cranston's first tea room, opened in 1878 at Argyle Street, made her name through the quality of its service and catering, and its artistic sense of décor. In 1888, she commissioned the young George Walton to carry out decorations as part of its refurbishment; in 1886 she opened the first of her Ingram Street premises.

Mackintosh entered the enlightened sphere of Miss Cranston's patronage in 1896, possibly introduced by Newbery. The following year, under Walton's direction, he created stencilled murals for the new development at Buchanan Street and furniture and light fittings for the expanded and redeveloped Argyle Street premises, again working under the overall design control of Walton, who was responsible for interior fittings and decoration. The high, oval-backed chair created by Mackintosh for the lunch room at Argyle Street represents the first true example of a 'Mackintosh chair'.

The collaboration between the two designers cannot have been an entirely happy one. Walton can be credited for introducing Arts and Crafts ideals to commercial Glasgow, and his delicate stencil patterns helped to define the tea-room style, generating the artistic ambience sought by his perceptive patron. Mackintosh, however, did not possess the type of creative personality which readily relinquishes control. By 1900, Walton had left Glasgow to set up business in London although he retained his Glasgow office, and Mackintosh had sole charge of Miss Cranston's projects.

Mackintosh's work at Ingram Street in 1900 encompassed the design of both furniture and decoration. Little direct evidence remains of this scheme, but the White Luncheon Room provided another striking example of the white interiors of this period. White enamelled paintwork emphasized the expanse of window and high ceiling; a mezzanine was added at the back, with coloured glass squares set into the balcony. A screen with leaded glass panels separated the lunch room from the entrance area. At either side of the room were two gesso panels, *The May Queen* by Margaret Macdonald and *The Wassail* by Mackintosh, accompanied by two beaten metal panels. Other metalwork included a lead-covered fireplace decorated with stylized plant motifs. The furniture, in dark-stained oak, included chairs with pierced back splats in two heights, one exceptionally high.

Detail from O Ye That Walk in Willow Wood (ABOVE), *a gesso panel created by Margaret Macdonald Mackintosh, c. 1903, for the Room de Luxe at the Willow Tea Rooms. The title is a line taken from a sonnet by Dante Gabriel Rossetti.*

The Room de Luxe (RIGHT) *is entered through a pair of elaborate stained glass doors. The form of the leaded design suggests the shape of a kimono, and features the familiar rose motif.*

Ingram Street was succeeded by the Willow Tea Rooms in 1903; following this supreme achievement, as Miss Cranston expanded and revamped her growing empire, Mackintosh's involvement in a variety of other interiors provides a fascinating chronicle of his design development. The 1906 Dutch Kitchen at Argyle Street was sleek and sophisticated despite its rather cosy theme, with the square as the principal decorative motif on linoleum, dados, pillars and furniture. Windsor chairs in emerald green provided a vivid colour accent against the graphic black and white. The design of the Oak Room at Ingram Street, with its three-sided balcony, coincided with Mackintosh's designs for the Library at the School of Art and featured the same expressed wooden construction, with wavy lines and chamfering as decorative elements on furniture and fittings. In 1911 Mackintosh was again at work at Ingram Street. The Blue or Chinese Room was a bold and unusually brightly coloured interior with severely rectilinear decoration in the form of latticework screens and panels; the Cloister Room, with its rippling bands of stencilled diaper patterns on the walls and strips of low relief crossing

Waitresses in the Room de Luxe. Miss Cranston was a perfectionist in all matters and reputedly vetted prospective members of staff by having them first wait upon her and her husband at home.

the barrel-vaulted plaster ceiling, displayed a striking adaptation of the 'waggon-chamfering' in the Library interior. There are indications that with these two interiors Mackintosh believed himself to be on the brink of a new design direction. Mackintosh's final work for Miss Cranston was the 1917 interior of a basement room, patriotically called 'The Dug-Out'. Here, shiny black decoration relieved by brightly coloured geometric shapes reflected his concurrent approach at Derngate.

Miss Cranston lost interest in her tea-room empire after 1917, when her husband, to whom she was devoted, suddenly died. Her long and successful dominance of the Glasgow tea-room business and her championing of the latest in design and décor made her a household word: 'quite Kate Cranstonish' was the local term for the refined, artistic and progressive. The Cranston tea rooms spawned countless imitators; although no other proprietor dared commission Mackintosh to design interiors, watered-down versions of the new style testified to its impact.

The Room de Luxe, recently restored, was designed as an exquisite setting for the refined ritual of taking tea. The effect of the long low casement window was repeated in the mirrored and stained glass wall panels which run round the perimeter of the room. Below the panels the walls were covered with purple silk stitched with beads.

'. . . [Miss Cranston's] new establishment fairly outshines all others in the matters of arrangement and colour . . .'

The Willow Tea Rooms opened in 1903 to breathless acclaim. Many who came to gawp or laugh stayed to admire; nothing quite so advanced or luxurious had ever been seen in Glasgow before.

IN THIS SINGLE TEA-ROOM PROJECT, MACKINTOSH WAS ABLE TO CREATE THE ARCHITECTURAL structure, interiors and their furnishings, controlling every aspect of the design, down to the white uniforms of the waitresses and their pink bead chokers. The building which took shape behind Mackintosh's tantalizing hoarding was situated in Glasgow's most fashionable street, Sauchiehall Street. The literal translation of the name, 'alley of the willows', provided an evocative and instantly sympathetic metaphor. The 'tea rooms' actually comprised three interconnected tea or dining rooms, the Room de Luxe, a billiard room and a smoking room, set on four levels.

The white exterior of the building is divided horizontally into two portions by a narrow projecting hood. Below this projection the front curves gently; above, one half of the façade is also curved. Above the square grid of the shop window front is a long casement window extending almost the full width of the building. With its graphic border of chequered squares, windows sparkling with mirrored glass inserts, decorative wrought ironwork and pristine finish, the Willow Tea Rooms must have presented a picture of startling modernity in 1903.

Internally, without employing the use of a single partition wall, Mackintosh created three distinct areas: the lofty front saloon, the rear saloon and the gallery linked to the ground floor by an open stair. As at Ingram Street, a white panelled screen with leaded glass inserts ushered customers from the entrance to the central cash desk, from which point they could either enter the front or rear rooms or go up the stair to the gallery and levels above. The ground floor extended to a height of 18 feet; the rear half of the building terminated at this level and was topped by a partially glazed roof beneath which the gallery was inserted. The skilful sequence from one distinct area to another, with views in every direction through open screens and stairs, displayed a truly modern manipulation of interior space. Above the front saloon on the first floor was the Room de Luxe; on the second floor were the smoking and billiard rooms.

The front saloon, or ladies' tea room, on the ground floor was largely decorated in white. Panelling extended up the wall to a height of about 7 feet; above this was a plaster relief frieze of stylized willow tree forms. Embroidered white panels hung at the windows; white cloths covered the tables. Dark-stained oak chairs, a Mackintosh interpretation of the traditional ladder-back, created a graphic counterpoint to the purity of the décor.

The back saloon, used for dining, was much darker, panelled in natural canvas with silvery stencilled designs of female figures and cabbage roses. In the centre of the room, under the open well lit by the overhead roof light, chairs were low and boxy; the fireplace at the rear of the space was fitted with three mirror panels to reflect the light.

The gallery above the back saloon was set out with tables and chairs along three sides of the central well. Eight columns supported the exposed beams of the coffered ceiling; over the gallery, sections of this egg-box construction were left open to admit light through the glazed parts of the roof.

A contemporary photograph of the Willow Tea Rooms, Sauchiehall Street. The pristine facade, with its graphic detail and glittering windows, presented a picture of startling modernity in 1903. The building occupies four storeys; the original interior comprised tea rooms, two dining rooms with a gallery and a billiard room.

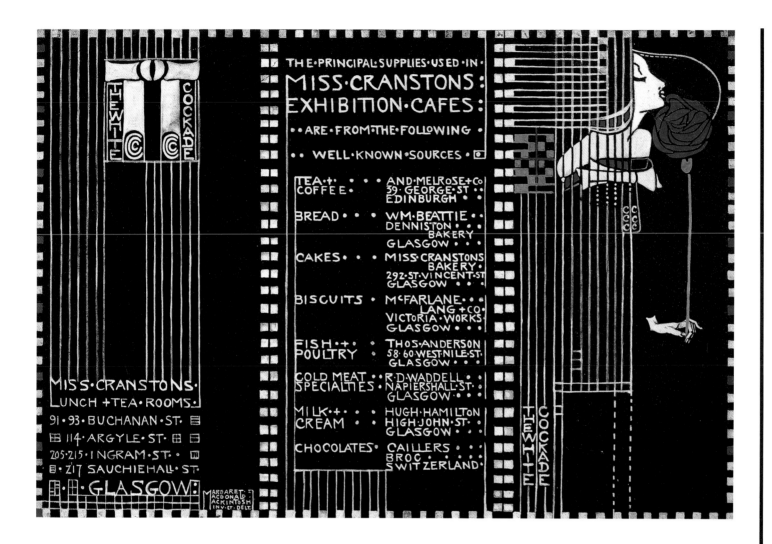

THE·PRINCIPAL·SUPPLIES·USED·IN·
MISS·CRANSTONS:
EXHIBITION·CAFES:
·•·ARE·FROM·THE·FOLLOWING·•
·•·WELL·KNOWN·SOURCES·

TEA·†· · ·	AND·MELROSE+Cº
COFFEE·	39·GEORGE·ST··
	EDINBURGH·•·
BREAD·•·•·	WM·BEATTIE·•·
	DENNISTON·•·•
	BAKERY
	GLASGOW·•··
CAKES·•·•	MISS·CRANSTONS
	BAKERY
	292·ST·VINCENT·ST
	GLASGOW·•··
BISCUITS·•	McFARLANE·•·
	LANG+Cº·
	VICTORIA·WORKS
	GLASGOW·•··
FISH·†··	THOS·ANDERSON
POULTRY·•	58·60·WEST·NILE·ST·
	GLASGOW·•··
COLD·MEAT·•	R·D·WADDELL·•·
SPECIALTIES	NAPIERSHALL·ST··
	GLASGOW·•·•
MILK·†·•·	HUGH·HAMILTON
CREAM·•·•	HIGH·JOHN·ST··
	GLASGOW·•·•
CHOCOLATES·	CAILLERS·•·•
	BROC·•·•·
	SWITZERLAND·

THE·WHITE·COCKADE

MISS·CRANSTONS·
LUNCH+TEA·ROOMS·
91·93·BUCHANAN·ST·
114·ARGYLE·ST·
205·215·INGRAM·ST··
217·SAUCHIEHALL·ST·
·GLASGOW·

MARGARET
MACDONALD
MACKINTOSH
INV·ET·DELT·

Margaret Macdonald Mackintosh designed this strikingly graphic menu for The White Cockade, *Miss Cranston's tea room and restaurant at the Glasgow Exhibition of 1911.*

The fourth side of the well formed a corridor flanked by a low glass and metalwork screen, through which the front saloon could be viewed. The staircase was also open, with fine steel rods taken up to the ceiling to form balusters. Between the balusters at the top were metal panels twisted into abstract shapes from which hung green glass balls – another reference to the willow tree theme.

On the ground floor, two large pieces of furniture served as spatial markers. One was a large semicircular chair, the lattice of its back forming a stylized tree, where the manageress sat to receive the waitresses' orders. This stood between the front and rear saloons, with its back towards an extraordinary wooden-framed construction in the front saloon, which supported a metal cage holding a huge glass bowl. The bowl was filled with test-tube containers, into each of which was placed a single flower.

The Room de Luxe on the first floor represents the most delicate and luxurious interior Mackintosh ever designed. The long casement window, with views over Sauchiehall Street, was enriched with a shimmering pattern of mirror glass shaped like willow leaves. Around the remainder of the room the effect was echoed in a frieze of mirror and purple and white leaded glass panels, above purple silk wall coverings stitched with beads. There were two heights of chairs, painted silver and upholstered in purple velvet, with purple glass inserts in the taller version. Elaborate entrance doors sparkled with glass, and an extravagant chandelier of glass baubles hung from the ceiling. On the wall opposite the fireplace was a gesso panel by Margaret Macdonald encrusted with glass beads and fragments of shell, which took as its theme lines from a sonnet by D. G. Rossetti: 'O ye, all ye that walk in Willowwood'. The Room de Luxe must certainly rank as one of the most exquisitely artistic surroundings ever created for the refined ritual of taking tea.

Derngate

78 Derngate, Northampton
Client: W. J. Bassett-Lowke
Designed: 1916–20

DERN-GATE

W J. BASSETT-LOWKE, MACKINTOSH'S LAST IMPORTANT CLIENT, WAS A MANUFACTURER OF SCALE models based in Northampton. Modern and progressive, he was well-informed about technological and design developments in Austria and Germany and keen to promote designers who shared his outlook. In 1914, when Bassett-Lowke was holidaying in Cornwall, a friend from Scotland extolled the work of 'artist architect' Mackintosh. Over a year later, after Bassett-Lowke had travelled to Glasgow and made contact with the Newberys, he traced Mackintosh to London.

Bassett-Lowke had acquired a small terraced property in Northampton which he wished to renovate in preparation for his marriage in 1917. His original intention had been to build a new house, but wartime restrictions on construction ruled this out. The commission could not have arrived at a better time for Mackintosh.

What Mackintosh was able to achieve at Derngate represented an entirely new design direction. New ideas, tried out more tentatively in the late tea-room interiors, were handled with great

The lounge hall at Derngate, in this contemporary photograph, was decorated in a vivid and dramatic fashion. The stepped forms of the fire surround anticipate Art Deco.

confidence and flair in this commission, where he completely abandoned the organic and vernacular motifs of his earlier work in favour of bold geometric patterning and a modern handling of architectural form. Nevertheless, Derngate was much smaller and more limited in scope than any of Mackintosh's previous domestic commissions, and can only provide a tantalizing indication of how he might have progressed given the opportunity to work on a larger scale.

78 Derngate was an early nineteenth-century brick Victorian terraced house, on a site that sloped steeply from front to back; there were three storeys at the front and an extra lower floor at ground level at the rear. At the front of the house, Mackintosh's alterations included substituting a bay window

for the existing sash window and providing a new front door with inset triangular panels of glass. At the rear of the house, Mackintosh created a small extension of striking modernity. The crisp white-rendered façade, with its use of balconies, both open and enclosed, and horizontal openings shielded with awnings, has all the functional simplicity of modernist houses constructed a decade or more later.

Inside, the main alteration was to move the staircase from its original location immediately to the left of the entrance to a central position between the front and rear rooms. The result was to increase the narrow hall to a 'lounge-hall'. The decoration of this room was frankly dramatic and mysterious. The walls, ceiling and furniture were painted black. Chequered bands of black and white squares suggested the effect of tree trunks around the room, and a decorative frieze, based on the theme of the triangle, was stencilled around the room, adding glowing touches of bright colour – silver-grey, yellow, vermilion, green, purple and blue. The central stair was screened from the room by a wooden divider, composed of open and closed squares. The carpet was black and white check, and the furniture was also based on the square or lattice motif. The stepped form of the fire surround echoed the treatment of the entrance on the west face of the School of Art.

Bassett-Lowke himself designed much of the furniture for the dining-room. Mackintosh papered the walls in a dark print outlined with strips of walnut; the ceiling and frieze were white. Fitted cupboards were installed on either side of the fireplace, and the fire surround was tiled. The master bedroom was papered in pale grey trimmed in mauve edging; the woodwork was white and furniture in grey sycamore was outlined in black inlay.

The guest bedroom, which was redesigned in 1919, was the most original interior of the entire scheme. Black and white striped paper extended behind the heads of the twin beds and was taken up over the ceiling to suggest a canopy. The outer stripe was ultramarine blue harness braid, secured by black-headed tacks. On either side of the main panel, two narrow panels of stripes swept across the ceiling to form a border at the top of the window. Striped curtains and bedspreads echoed the theme.

The oak furniture which Mackintosh designed for his room was exceptionally simple, the plain wood finish decorated with a narrow trim of blue squares stencilled on a black strip. The theme of the square was again ever-present, in cut-outs in the top rail of the beds, as lattice ends for stools, in the small square ebonized handles. Strong and well-constructed (Bassett-Lowke often made use of immigrant craftsmen from Germany and the guest bedroom furniture was made by German civil prisoners of war on the Isle of Man), the furniture Mackintosh created for Derngate is especially prophetic of later trends in design.

The Derngate guest bedroom, designed in 1919 and reconstructed as part of The Mackintosh House at the Hunterian Gallery, is an interior of striking originality. Black and white stripes edged in ultramarine braid were taken up behind the bedheads and over the ceiling as a canopy. Two bands of stripes went on to form a border framing the window on the opposite side. The Derngate furniture was well-constructed; Mackintosh's client Bassett-Lowke used immigrant German craftsmen to execute the designs. Much of the furniture was later installed at the house Bassett-Lowke commissioned from Peter Behrens.

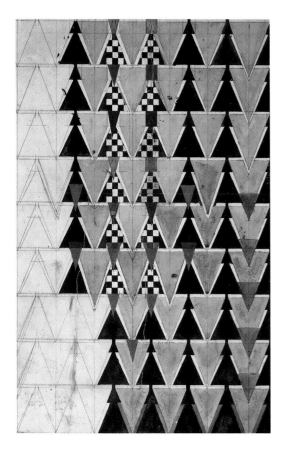

Mackintosh executed a number of other small commissions for Bassett-Lowke and his circle during this time. At Bassett-Lowke's cottage outside Northampton he decorated and furnished the dining-room. A pattern of dark squares and light oblongs was stencilled around the top of the dark-papered walls. At the corners of the room, vertical 'ladders' were created by varying the position of three different stencils to form abstract linear patterns.

In 1920 Mackintosh was asked back to Derngate to redecorate the lounge-hall in a lighter fashion, as Mrs Bassett-Lowke in particular had begun to find the severe black geometries a little oppressive. Accordingly, he painted the woodwork grey and added a smaller stencilled frieze which Bassett-Lowke later repeated in his study at New Ways, the house he commissioned from Behrens in 1924. Much of the furniture Mackintosh designed for Bassett-Lowke was also installed there. The Derngate guest bedroom has now been reconstructed at the Hunterian Art Gallery in Glasgow.

Design for the hall stencilling at Derngate, 1916. The bold chevron motif and use of primary colour make a contrast to the organic and more delicately coloured stencilled decoration of The Hill House. Eventually Mrs Bassett-Lowke is said to have found the dark geometries too oppressive and the lounge-hall was repainted in a lighter fashion.

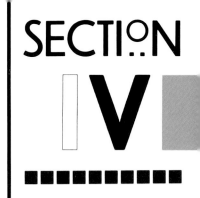

ELEMENTS OF THE STYLE

ELEMENTS OF THE STYLE

It is difficult for the architect to draw a fixed line between the architecture of the house and its furniture. The conception of an interior must naturally include the furniture which is to be used in it, and this naturally leads to the conclusion that the architect should design the chairs and tables as well as the house itself.

BAILLIE SCOTT, IN AN ARTICLE IN *THE STUDIO* IN 1895, DESCRIBED THE APPROACH WHICH MACKINTOSH adopted whenever the opportunity arose. In domestic commissions such as Windyhill, The Hill House and, to a certain extent, Derngate, house, landscape, interiors, decoration, furniture and fittings were not individual elements to be conceived in isolation, but aspects of the whole. Few architects since Robert Adam have displayed such an all-embracing artistic vision.

Unfortunately, opportunities for Mackintosh to design both a building and its contents were few and far between. For much of his career, he had to make do with adapting an existing house or interior to provide a setting for his design ideas. In his own homes at Mains Street and Southpark Avenue and in many of the tea rooms he created for Miss Cranston, he proved himself to be supremely skilled at manipulating the architectural qualities of interior space, transforming unpromising nineteenth-century rooms into interiors of startling originality. Because these interiors were so different from anything that had gone before, it was inevitable that Mackintosh should also design everything they contained.

The dining room fireplace at The Hill House has a cement surround and simple border of four-square motifs in inlaid tile. Mackintosh fireplaces were among the most radical elements of his interiors, a far cry from the ornate marble or cast-iron and tile examples typical of the period. Their uncompromising geometries, fully integrated within the proportional system of the interiors, anticipate the minimal detailing of equivalent features in the work of designers of the Modern Movement.

INTER-■■IOR DEC☉R ATION

MACKINTOSH IS BEST KNOWN FOR HIS WHITE INTERIORS, ROOMS WHICH WERE OVERWHELMINGLY white but not merely so. But white decoration was not new or original to Mackintosh. Godwin's white interior for Oscar Wilde in 1884 is an early example of the use of white to convey a mood of heightened artistic refinement. Even before this date, William Morris was a champion of the virtues of plain whitewashed walls: 'honest whitewash . . . on which sun and shadow play so pleasantly . . .' Plain distempered walls at Red House excited much comment; the panelled drawing-room at Morris's country house, Kelmscott Manor, was also painted white. At Clouds, the Wiltshire house designed by Philip Webb for the Wyndhams in the late 1880s, Morris tapestries and fabrics were hung against a pure white background.

To the Victorians, the use of white in the interior was shocking and extreme. White was the colour of utility, of privies, service rooms and cowsheds; it was emphatically not the background for genteel living. By the end of the century, however, even at the level of popular taste, there was a clear indication of a shift towards lighter, brighter interiors.

At first, white found a more general acceptance as a colour for bedrooms. During the latter part of the nineteenth century, the need for cleanliness and hygiene in the home preoccupied many writers on household subjects. Light and fresh air were more positively sought in the interior, no longer ruthlessly excluded by layers of heavy window drapery. The bedroom, where vermin could lurk in dusty hangings and furnishings, was the first area in the home where this desire for a clean sweep was expressed. Many design historians have also linked the use of white with the emergence of electric lighting, which began to come into use around this time. Electric light was not only brighter and more revealing, it also meant that interior surfaces no longer had to be treated in such a way as to disguise the inevitable discoloration caused by fumes from gas jets.

Mackintosh's first recorded use of white was in a bedroom he designed and furnished for the publisher J. Maclehose at Westdel, Glasgow, in 1898. The following year, white was more radically employed in the Director's room at the School of Art. A year later, at Mains Street, white was used in the drawing-room and studio as well as the main bedroom.

Mackintosh's use of white undoubtedly reflected his instinct for simplicity and his delight in natural light. His white interiors, however, were neither clinical nor utilitarian. On the contrary, these rooms did much to establish white as a colour of supreme artistic refinement, even luxury, an association exploited very successfully over twenty years later in the work of designer Jean-Michel Frank and society decorators such as Syrie Maugham and Elsie de Wolfe.

Looking down to the curved half-landing on the main staircase at The Hill House. The extended newel post with its 'mortarboard' capping, a feature derived from the work of Mackmurdo, provides a visual link between levels. The tall narrow staircase windows spill light down the stairs, leading the eye upwards from the dark entrance hall. Mackintosh staircases were the means of expressing spatial volume, revealing what has been called 'the interpenetration of spaces' in the manner of traditional Japanese construction. In the design of such features, Mackintosh reveals a mastery of the dynamics of space.

Mackintosh's white rooms were not all white. The 'white' itself was closer to ivory and might be offset by the neutral shades of soft grey-brown carpeting and natural linen or painted canvas. Colour was not banished, but limited to small touches in glass or enamel panels, in embroidery or stencilled designs. In the white interiors, all woodwork was also enamelled white and much of the furniture painted white; light was diffused by plain muslin screens at the window and simple unlined white curtains. The overwhelming effect was one of smoothness, softness and intimacy, even, some would suggest, of subtle eroticism.

On the practical level, the maintenance of these interiors must have proved a greater problem in a grimy, sooty industrial city at the turn of the century than the equivalent decoration would today. Smoke from open fireplaces and fumes from gas lighting would have posed a constant threat to these immaculate surfaces, despite the best housekeeping efforts. The Mackintoshes were both exceptionally fastidious: Margaret, apparently, found it no hardship to paint in an all-white studio. Like most households of that period, they employed a maid; even so, Margaret was known to tackle the occasional stubborn smudge or mark herself with a little warm olive oil. But perhaps it is not altogether surprising that white decoration failed to become more generally popular until electricity and clean forms of heating became more universally available.

Mackintosh's white interiors generally formed part of a sequence of spaces. In other rooms and adjoining areas, his basic decorative formula relied on the contrast between white or neutral shades and dark woodwork, panelling or paper, relieved by small areas of more colourful pattern, often in the form of stencilling. This restricted palette was an important means of achieving unity, but was never bland or predictable.

In dining-rooms, a preferred treatment was to cover the walls below the picture rail in coarse brown wrapping paper. Woodwork here was often stained dark or black and waxed, although the frieze and ceiling were generally painted white. Dark walls created the moody, mysterious atmosphere Mackintosh felt appropriate for dining and helped to focus attention on the table. As an alternative to being papered, the walls might be panelled in dark-stained or natural wood, a treatment also adopted for the 'masculine' interiors of libraries or studies. The dining-room Mackintosh designed for Hugo, Brückmann, publisher of *Dekorative Kunst*, in Munich in 1898, is the first known example of this decorative formula.

Entrances were similarly dark, with brown papered or white papered or painted areas of wall graphically outlined with dark-stained strips of wood to form the impression of panelling. The sombre

The hall table at The Hill House, made in 1904, is in varnished oak. This table and its accompanying chairs are the only pieces of furniture Mackintosh designed for the house which are not painted or stained. The square cutouts on the legs echo the squares which pierce the aprons of the chairs, and convey an impression of solidity and strength by revealing the thickness of the wood. The candlesticks on the table were also designed by Mackintosh for The Hill House in 1904. Each has a square base, and four tapering legs which support shallow cups. Their futuristic form displays an astonishing modernity.

decoration of the hall had the effect of leading the eye on to light spilling down the stairwell and provided a dramatic foil for the pure white interiors awaiting discovery further on.

The relatively narrow tonal range of Mackintosh's decoration belies the diversity of effect. The progression from dark to light, outer room to inner sanctum, was orchestrated with infinite care and, on the face of it, with the simplest of means.

■ ■ ■

Proportion and Architectural Detail

**INTER-
■■IOR
DECOR
ATION**

MACKINTOSH'S RADICAL DECORATIVE IDEAS WERE CONCEIVED IN THE CONTEXT OF A NEW WAY OF proportioning interior space. In situations where he was unable to create the fabric of the building, decorative effects were not simply applied to an existing framework, the perceived scale of the room itself was altered in a variety of ways.

In the Victorian period, the basic proportions of the interior derived from the classical model. The wall area, treated as a stylized form of a temple façade, was subdivided by a deep skirting board (baseboard), a dado rail about a third of the way up the wall, a picture rail, a decorative frieze and a cornice. In many instances, the dado might be treated in a different decorative manner from the larger portion of wall above, usually in a more robust fashion to reduce the effect of wear and tear. Ceilings were high and enriched with plasterwork mouldings and central roses (medallions).

By the late nineteenth century, Arts and Crafts designers had brought about a shift in these proportional arrangements. The frieze gradually became deeper, with the picture rail dropped down to align with the head of the door frame or architrave. Alternatively, a panelled dado might be taken up to this level, but the effect was the same reversal of the traditional arrangement. The result was to lower the apparent height of the room and introduce a strong horizontal emphasis.

Mackintosh took these new proportions a step closer to the modern concept of interior space, with its minimal detailing and plain expanses of surface. In his interiors, the cosy rusticity of Arts and Crafts rooms is entirely missing and the crisp horizontality becomes a means for unifying structure with surface and finish.

The classic example was his transformation of a high-ceilinged Victorian room at Southpark Avenue, where a broad flat picture rail tied together the heads of windows, doors and openings, running like a band to encircle the entire room. Above the rail, a new portion of wall taken across the top of the bay window reduced its height. The frieze and ceiling were resolutely plain, stripped of their original classically inspired plasterwork moulding.

In his architectural work, the same proportional strategies are in evidence. A deep picture shelf or rail is often the principal organizing element, linking the heads of doorways or window frames, marking the extent of built-in shelving or serving as the upper limit for stencilled panels. Light fittings are hung so that their lower edge also aligns with the defining feature of the picture rail. The result is visually to suspend the decorative and furnished elements of the interior like an inner skin within the white structural shell, emphasizing the tension between the two.

■ ■ ■

Decorative Detail

INTER-
■■IOR
DECOR
ATION

STENCILLING WAS ONE OF THE PRIME MEANS BY WHICH MACKINTOSH INTRODUCED COLOUR AND pattern into his interiors. It is easy to appreciate why this technique held such an appeal. Stencilling can be applied to a variety of different surfaces, from paint, paper and textiles to woodwork; it is both an economic and highly versatile form of decoration. One-off or limited runs of printed paper or fabric are rarely cost-effective, but well-executed stencilling can offer an almost identical effect. For a designer such as Mackintosh, who used decorative motif as a means of unifying different elements in the interior, stencilling served his purposes admirably well.

The clean outlines of a cut stencil provided an ideal medium for the translation of graphic motifs. The first Mackintosh stencils to attract widespread attention, at the Buchanan Street Tea Rooms, appeared to many observers to be a direct interpretation of his poster work. In the domestic interiors, the stencilling is necessarily on a much smaller scale, but it never descended to the level of tentative trimming often seen today, where wispy tendrils trail half-heartedly round door and window frames. Instead, it formed part of the entire interior composition, organized in bold vertical bands or banner-like panels. In contrast to the enveloping, layered richness of Victorian and Edwardian interiors, the rhythm of these repeated motifs, set off by expanses of plain background, served as an abstraction of decorative pattern. Stencilling was never used to cover a surface completely and in that sense stand in for a printed finish such as wallpaper or fabric.

Stencilled designs often combined the organic motif of the rose with the geometric element of the square. Various commentators have interpreted the rose as a feminine symbol, emblematic of creativity and love, or as a more direct reference to the inspiration of Mackintosh's wife Margaret, or of Scotland and Glasgow in particular. As a summary of nature, the rose or rosebud was evidently a potent symbol for Mackintosh during the middle years of his career. Enclosed by entwining thickets of thorny stems or more

Stained glass lights in the door of Studio 45, The Glasgow School of Art. Stylized rosebuds – emblematic of Glasgow, love, creativity – feature widely in the decorative repertoire of the School. In a defiantly plain building, such small touches of colour define places of importance.

abstractly employed as a punctuation point, the circular form of the rose stands in opposition to the solid, structural square. In the hall at The Hill House, the stencilled frieze combines geometric and organic motifs in a more abstract way and introduces the muted colours of green, rose, blue and mauve which are picked up in the design of the carpet.

Colour is also evident in glowing panels of enamel, coloured or leaded glass inset in doors or pieces of furniture. The presence of such lustrous details, in the words of one critic, brings 'a note of expectancy' to thresholds and places of transition. The role of these small touches of colour to generate surprise and anticipation can be seen in their hidden presence within cabinets, desks and cupboards, or on the glazed panels of bookcases or doors, announcing a concealed richness. The interplay between colour and light was also richly exploited. The rhythm of stairs was marked by panels of coloured glass; colour accentuated the semi-transparency of timber screens; coloured squares set into picture rails where they crossed windows were backlit by light.

Until the later years, Mackintosh's colours were largely the subtle shades of green, rose, purple, silver and gold, the tertiary colours seen as advanced and progressive in Aesthetic circles. The contemporary identification of green and purple with women's suffrage was particularly strong and may have provided a resonant symbolism for their use in Mackintosh decoration, as some critics have suggested. The whole question of women's role in society and female emancipation was a burning contemporary issue, and the Glasgow Style was notable for its many active women participants. The Mackintoshes, through their friendship with Patrick Geddes, also had an interest in the Theosophist movement, whose followers idealized the female as the creative, spiritual, innovative force. Although some of these philosophical connections may at first seem far-fetched, Mackintosh was simply not a designer whose work was ever deficient in meaning.

■　■　■

FURN-
ITURE

MACKINTOSH'S NAME IS POPULARLY SYNONYMOUS WITH THE PURE GRAPHIC QUALITY OF HIS ebonized high-backed chairs. These designs, with their intersecting planes, gridded detail or square motifs, have become icons of modern design. But chairs were only one, albeit important, element of Mackintosh's prolific output as a furniture designer. During his career he produced over 400 different designs for a huge range of pieces, from clocks to hatstands, wardrobes to light fittings. Furniture, its design and placement, was integral to the way he conceived interior space.

Mackintosh furniture varies in style as well as type. The attenuated form of his most famous designs, such as the 1903 ladder-back chair for the Hill House bedroom, dates from the middle period. Earlier

In a corner of the drawing room at The Hill House, the decorative motif of the rose can be seen on the fixed wall sconce, wall stencilling and the embroidered shade of the standard lamp, giving unity to the overall design. The standard lamp is in sycamore and dates from 1905.

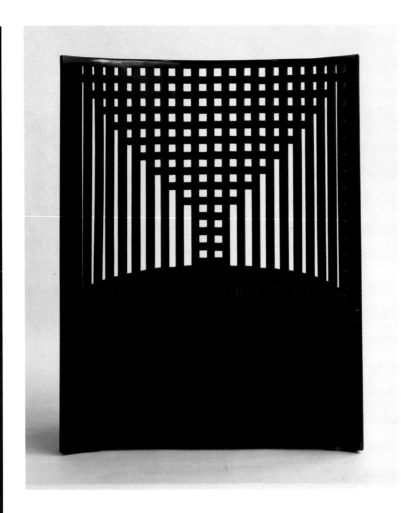

The curved lattice-back chair (1904), created for the Willow Tea Rooms, is one of Mackintosh's most elegant and original designs, with its wide sweeping back detailed in the form of a stylized willow tree. The chair had the prosaic function of providing a place for the tea room manageress to sit while taking orders. Positioned in the centre of the tea room, it served as a screen between front and rear areas.

work is often decorated with organic motifs, while the last pieces, designed for Derngate, display a severe modernity.

Mackintosh probably began to design furniture around 1893. Some of his first pieces were produced for a firm of Glasgow cabinet-makers, Guthrie and Wells. These designs, mainly for wardrobes and washstands, were solid and simple, with bold metal handles and hinges in the Arts and Crafts manner. By 1896, some of the characteristic features of his early work were beginning to emerge. The oak hall settle that he exhibited at the Arts and Crafts Society Exhibition of 1896 is decorated with a stencilled design of plants on the back-rest and incorporates a repoussé lead panel portraying three peacocks. Organic motifs were present in all of his work for many years after. In the furniture designs, such decoration was at first applied and subsequently integrated in a more sculptural way.

This 1904 writing cabinet, exhibited in the studio of The Mackintosh House, is one of a version of three similar designs prepared for Walter Blackie and was made for Mackintosh's own use. Among the most sumptuous pieces Mackintosh ever created, the desk is of ebonized mahogany with various inlays of pearwood, mother-of-pearl, ivory and glass. The interior of the desk is fitted with pigeonholes and a sliding writing surface; when the doors are open, the desk takes on the 'kimono' form typical of many such pieces. The Blackie writing desk, which varies slightly from this example, was recently sold at auction for nearly £800,000.

The first extensive furniture commission was for Miss Cranston's Argyle Street Tea Rooms in 1897. Made of oak, dark-stained or in a natural finish, these pieces are strong and sturdy, with some carved decoration, but otherwise displaying a robust simplicity in keeping with their function. Mackintosh designed a range of different pieces, from low armchairs to tables for playing dominoes, from a hatstand to an upholstered settee.

The striking exception to these plain and often heavy designs was a high-backed chair, the first Mackintosh ever designed. In dark-stained oak, with a stylized cut-out of a flying bird in the oval back rail, the chair was designed for the central tables at the tea rooms, where its height would serve as a way both of defining the room and of providing a sense of intimacy and enclosure for diners. Mackintosh used a version of this same design in the dining-rooms of his own homes.

Designed for the Mains Street drawing room in 1900, this white-painted oak bookcase (RIGHT) *features elegant leaded glass panels of organic design. The two cabinets flank an open magazine rack.*

The studio fireplace at 78 Southpark Avenue (LEFT) *incorporated the grate from the drawing room at 120 Mains Street, one of the many fittings the Mackintoshes transferred from their former home. The T-shaped grate is based on a traditional design. Above the fireplace is a gesso panel entitled* The White Rose and the Red Rose *by Margaret Macdonald in 1902.*

Another new departure can be seen in the white-painted bedroom furniture of 1898, designed for the publisher Maclehose at Westdel. The hard white enamelled surface of these pieces enabled Mackintosh to treat wood in a more fluid, sculptural way, with gentle curves and sculptural decoration suggesting a more plastic medium. The high Argyle Street chair represents the first clear move away from the traditions of Arts and Crafts artisanship; these designs show a determined progress in the same direction. The coats of white paint served to hide the natural grain of the wood and conceal construction – on both accounts a 'dishonesty' in basic Arts and Crafts terms. The use of white paint enabled Mackintosh to explore an entirely new style of furniture design but also hid the constructional

133

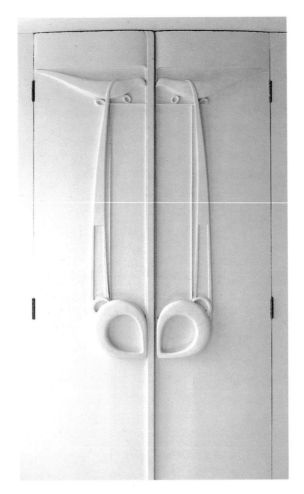

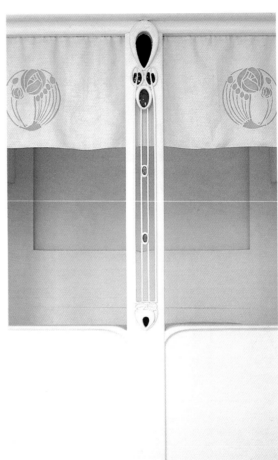

One of a pair of large wardrobes, designed for Mains Street in 1900, this piece (FAR LEFT) features fine raised details in the form of birds, which seem moulded rather than carved from the smooth white painted surface.

The four-poster bed from the Mains Street flat (LEFT) was the first that Mackintosh designed. Like the rest of the bedroom furniture, the bed is made of oak, painted white, with inset coloured glass.

faults that inevitably arose when the new style was achieved by ignoring the innate structural limitations of wood.

Much of the furniture at the Mains Street flat was also painted white. A spectacular bookcase in the drawing-room had intricate leaded glass panels; in the bedroom the white-painted four-poster bed featured fine carved detail and coloured glass inserts, while a large double wardrobe was also decorated with carving in the form of stylized birds. The sculptural possibilities of the new style are strikingly in evidence in the design of the bedroom cheval mirror, with its graceful sweeping curved uprights. At Mains Street, Mackintosh also installed a white-painted version of the high-backed chair he designed for the Ingram Street Tea Rooms, an elegant design with back splats pierced in a pattern of squares.

One of a pair of display cabinets designed in 1902 for Mrs Jessie Rowat, the mother of Fra Newbery's wife, Jessie, and made for Mackintosh's own use. The interior faces of the cupboard doors are decorated with stylized female figures holding large rosebuds. The pieces were exhibited at the Moscow Exhibition of 1903.

Some of the most delicate of Mackintosh's white-painted furniture was created for Mrs Rowat at Kingsborough Gardens. An oval side table of 1902, which he reproduced for his own use, has flat legs placed in such a way as to suggest that they form a continuation of the table top. Elegantly curved, with oval cut-outs and decorative splays of wood, it is difficult indeed to remember that the piece is actually fashioned from oak. The design was exhibited at Turin, along with an exceptionally tall chair with a tapering back which attracted the enthusiastic admiration of Fritz Wärndorfer, for whom Mackintosh was to design the celebrated Music Salon.

The furniture Mackintosh designed for the Willow Tea Rooms a year later was both wide-ranging and superbly innovative. The scope of the commission allowed him to embrace every detail, from cutlery to light fittings, although his designs for chairs are justifiably most famous. In the Room de Luxe, the sumptuous high-backed chair was painted silver and inset with nine panels of purple glass. In contrast to the gentle curves of this design, the ladder-back chair for the front saloon is a subtle reworking of a traditional form, the simple runged back apparently intended as another reminder of the willow tree theme. Of all the Willow Tea Room designs, perhaps the most beautiful is the semicircular order desk chair, the lattice pattern of the back forming a stylized tree. Designed for the prosaic purpose of providing a place for the tea room manageress to sit and receive orders from the waitresses, the chair also served as a screen and spatial divider between front and rear saloons.

Silver-plated cutlery designed by Mackintosh for the Willow Tea Rooms. The Italian firm Sabattini has been sub-licensed by Cassina to produce reproductions of these designs, together with vases, candlesticks, carafes and trays.

Mackintosh always paid careful attention to the practical needs of a household. An early example of fitted kitchen storage, these pantry cupboards at The Hill House with their heart-shaped cutouts and latticed door fronts, are as handsome in their way as the more famous pieces elsewhere in the house. Mackintosh spent time learning the habits and tastes of the Blackie family before designing The Hill House, and his loving attention to detail attests to the accuracy of his observations. The west-facing kitchen windows provide good afternoon light at a time when the family cook would be preparing the evening meal.

By 1903 Mackintosh was beginning to move away from the exaggerated delicacy of the white-painted furniture, and organic motifs were superseded by more rigorous geometries. The square or lattice is prominent in the design of much of the furniture for The Hill House. One of the best-known examples is the high-backed chair, designed for the main bedroom. Made in ebonized oak, with a simple upholstered seat, the chair stands almost as high as a person and its ladder-back extends right down to ground level. The suggestion of a head-rest is provided by a gridded upper portion. In the original surroundings, a pair of these chairs were precisely placed to serve as a visual anchor to the pristine white decoration, demarcating the two separate areas of the room.

Also at The Hill House, the hall table and chair in varnished oak were among the most robust pieces Mackintosh had designed since the Argyle Street commission. The square motif was handled in a bold fashion and the overriding impression is of strength and solidity.

One of the finest pieces Mackintosh ever created was the writing-desk he designed for Walter Blackie in 1904. Mackintosh's desks and display cabinets tended to be the most luxurious and decorative pieces he produced; this ebonized mahogany writing cabinet, with its mother-of-pearl inlay

and leaded glass panel, is probably his most successful of this type. The interior is fitted with pigeon-holes and has a sliding writing surface. The desk was made by Alexander Martin, one of two local tradesmen whom Mackintosh used on a regular basis (Francis Smith was the other); he was paid £20 ($30) 15s 6d ($1.20) for the finished piece. In 1994 the writing-desk sold at auction for £793,500 ($1,230,000).

Blackie was unable to commission as much furniture as Mackintosh would have hoped and certainly few pieces of the quality of the writing cabinet. His publishing business suffered a financial crisis around the time The Hill House was completed, and although Mackintosh executed a number of designs for the house several years later, only a few rooms were completely furnished with his work. One piece from this later date was the table for the drawing-room (1908), a masterful play on the square. A solid square top rests on an intersecting network of squares, a complex and highly sophisticated rhythmic composition.

At Hous'hill, the home of Miss Cranston and her husband Major Cochrane, Mackintosh had a much freer rein. He designed much more furniture here than at The Hill House, and although the house and its interior fittings were demolished after a fire in 1933, Miss Cranston had long since moved away and some of the pieces of furniture have survived. This commission saw Mackintosh concentrate more fully on geometric forms of the square or lattice, and much of the furniture is quite severe. Woods such as maple and sycamore, which have a finer grain than oak, were used to give

This elegant little table (TOP LEFT) *was made for the main bedroom at Windyhill in 1901. Like much Mackintosh furniture of this period, the grain of the wood, oak, is disguised under layers of smooth white paint.*

By 1904, when Mackintosh was engaged in the design of interiors and furniture for Miss Cranston at Hous'hill, he had virtually abandoned the organic references and decoration of his earlier work in favour of pure geometry. These oak chairs with chequered back rests (TOP)*, designed for the Blue Bedroom at Hous'hill, are among his simplest. The vertical rails of the back rest extend down below the seat to meet the rear stretcher.*

sharper edges, and the grain of the wood was left exposed. With its slender curving back rails, an armchair designed in 1904 for the drawing-room is one of Mackintosh's most refined pieces.

The Derngate furniture, which marks the final phase of Mackintosh's career, is the most radically simple and severe of his entire output. The lattice-work is bold, and there is a greater reliance on unbroken planes of wood and solidity of construction; the exposed grain of the wood is used to contribute decorative interest. Only in the black lounge-hall was the furniture lacquered black, elsewhere the wood was left in a natural finish. Squares of mother-of-pearl or a new synthetic material called Erinoid provide graphic definition on clock faces, wardrobe doors and mirror frames. Blue squares stencilled on a fine black strip edge the supremely plain oak pieces designed for the guest bedroom in 1919, the last furniture Mackintosh was ever to design. The Derngate pieces were much better made than their Glasgow counterparts, since Bassett-Lowke had them constructed by his own skilled employees, as well as by immigrant craftsmen from Germany. Both in strength and simplicity the Derngate furniture points to a new stylistic direction, a path of development which Mackintosh unhappily was never given the opportunity to pursue.

Mackintosh's furniture designs, upon which so much of his contemporary fame rests, constitute a remarkable body of work by any standard. In the best of these pieces the artist meets the architect in a particularly gratifying synthesis; a chair can be at once a summary of an entire architectural approach and a work of sculpture in its own right. The use and arrangement of furniture was not merely functional for Mackintosh, it was part of the way in which space was articulated and expressed; and if individual pieces occasionally failed to perform practically, it was because their visual function was ultimately of greater importance and interest. In the absence of greater opportunities to build, the richness of his architectural imagination found some expression in the progression embodied by these designs.

■　■　■

FITTINGS & FIXTURES

AS WELL AS FURNITURE, MACKINTOSH DESIGNED A HOST OF OTHER ANCILLARY FITTINGS AND INTERIOR fixtures. The care and attention he devoted to such relatively insignificant items — cutlery, candlesticks, hat racks and coat racks, billiard scoreboards, vases and umbrella stands — testify to the thoroughness of his approach. Many working drawings for such details survive, all executed with his characteristic precision; the effect, naturally, was to provide his interior schemes with the highest degree of unity and coherence.

Clocks were among the most beautifully realized of these smaller pieces. The clock designed for the Willow Tea Rooms in 1903 has squares bordering the clock face and a latticed case. In the

The 1903 design of the washstand from the main bedroom at The Hill House reveals a transition from the early organic motifs to the new geometric style. Both elements are expressed in the decorative glass inset in the doors and on the mirrored splashback.

entrance hall at The Hill House, the wall-mounted clock is even more restrained and elegant in design, with a metal face painted with Roman numerals organized as a square. Another clock design for The Hill House, dating from 1905, consists of a black cube containing the works supported on sixteen square pillars. Mackintosh took a similar approach in the design of clocks for Derngate. In one example, dating from 1917, the clock face is yet more radical and modern, with a pattern of domino dots standing in for numerals.

Light fittings were understandably of interest to a designer who was so acutely aware of the quality of light in the interior. A typical Mackintosh design was a pendant square metal shade surmounted by a curved metal top to reflect the light downwards. Clusters of these fittings were used in the gas-lit Mains Street interiors, but proved equally successful as shades for electric light. Mackintosh designs for light fittings display ingenious variations on a decorative theme, but many follow the basic format of the open lantern of metalwork or leaded glass. There are wall-mounted lanterns in the bedroom at The Hill House, while the large fittings for the hall lights, with their metal framework and panels of opaque glass, have a Japanese quality. The metal light fittings designed in 1900 for the Director's room at the School of Art (but only recently executed and installed) comprise open metal lanterns with nine square cut-outs wrapped around each corner. Most dramatic of all are the hanging lamps in the Library, thirteen angular steel fittings with coloured inserts hung at staggered heights to create a central pool of light.

The fireplace provided Mackintosh with the opportunity to create a glowing focus of decorative and symbolic interest. An early example was the fireplace Mackintosh designed in 1900 for Dunglass Castle, Bowling, the home of the Macdonalds. Here, an existing marble fireplace was covered by a new wooden structure which integrated the hearth into the new long, low interior proportions. The surround was rendered and the mantelpiece was flanked by pigeon-holes. The sweeping sculptural curves of the design were repeated in the form of the Mains Street fireplace, which was also painted white, a masterpiece of elegance and simplicity. Its wide mantelshelf was used to display vases and pictures; the grate was based on a traditional hob form.

Another fireplace design from around this date was created for the drawing-room at Kingsborough Gardens, the home of Mrs Rowat. A timber surround projected out from the wall to the depth of the hearth. Pigeon-holes were set into the curved planes of its cheeks, and the rendered surround was decorated with nine square blue tiles. A central strengthening bracket was carved in an organic form and decorated with coloured glass. The 1903 white-painted fireplace in the front saloon at the

One of Mackintosh's most accomplished designs, this fireplace dates from 1900 and was originally made for the drawing room at Mains Street. When the Mackintoshes moved to Southpark Avenue, they took the fireplace with them and installed it there, making certain adaptations to suit the new setting. The long low lines, shallow smooth curves and beautifully judged proportions of the surround make it a fitting focal point for an exquisitely detailed room. The lead clad fender incorporates two fireside seats for the Mackintoshes' cats.

Willow Tea Rooms also featured square tiles set in the cement render of the surround; the wooden mantelpiece was decorated with four carved motifs, possibly intended as light-fittings. The fireplace in the back saloon was a variation on this theme, with a border of square tiles in the surround and three niches inlaid with faceted mirror glass over the mantelshelf.

Every fireplace at The Hill House plays an important compositional role within the context of its setting. This is well demonstrated in the drawing-room, where the fireplace is set into a shallow curved recess with three square niches at either side. The mantelshelf extends to meet the base of the upper niches with consummate elegance and economy. The surround is tiled in mosaic and features five drop-shaped panels of coloured and mirror glass. Above the mantelshelf is a recess holding a gesso panel by Margaret Macdonald. At Windyhill, the drawing-room fireplace had been treated in a similar manner, with a rich gold mosaic surround inset with rose motifs.

In The Hill House library, the fireplace forms part of the practical fitting out of this working room. The mosaic surround is framed by oak, with a pair of narrow recessed windows above at either side. A row of pigeon-holes extends across the top of the surround; beneath the mantelshelf at either side are incorporated a pair of small pull-down writing-desks. The attenuated design of the hall fireplace serves to link various levels at the entrance; while in the main bedroom, the fire surround is polished steel inset with panels of coloured mosaic, forming a glittering focus for the all-white decoration.

The sheer artistry of these fireplaces, their modernity of form and proportion and the manner in which each design constitutes an individual response to a particular location, stand in great contrast to the cumbersome cast-iron or marble edifices typical of the period. While later Mackintosh designs, such as the hall fireplace at Derngate (1917), seem to anticipate the decorative motifs of Art Deco; even the much earlier examples, with their refinement of ornament, horizontal emphasis and use of unusual materials, are more progressive and original than any other equivalent feature produced by contemporary designers or architects.

■ ■ ■

FURNI SHINGS & TEXTILES

MACKINTOSH INTERIORS WERE SPARSELY ARRANGED AND FURNISHED, AND THE RESTRAINT EXTENDED to the use of fabric, either at the window or covering individual pieces of furniture. Today we are accustomed to such simplicity, but at the turn of the century the effect was highly radical and innovative. Edwardian interiors were lighter than their Victorian counterparts, but by no means under-furnished. Curtain headings may have been simpler and softer, but there were still layers of fabric at the window and a medley of patterns displayed on loose covers, upholstery and floor coverings. Chintzes and other figured or floral prints were much in evidence in ordinary households at this time.

A polished steel fire surround inset with mosaic panels provides a scintillating focus in the main bedroom at The Hill House. The high-backed couch set in the alcove beside the fire provides a place for Mrs Blackie to entertain her friends.

Mackintosh relished light, and the window treatments he devised were simple in the extreme. In the white interiors, he often made use of muslin panels or screens to soften or filter strong daylight. Curtains, which might be hung from the picture rail, as at Mains Street or Southpark Avenue, were often little more than unlined flat panels of off-white fabric, minimally embroidered with appliquéd organic motifs and graphically edged with a narrow black trim. Bed hangings were treated in a similar fashion, enriched with stencilled or embroidered motifs.

On the floor, Mackintosh favoured a muted grey-brown wall-to-wall carpeting or plain polished wood. In the entrance hall at The Hill House, the carpet has a border of squares which repeat the colours of the wall stencilling. At Southpark Avenue, according to Dr Howarth, Mackintosh at one time experimented with a blue sized sailcloth floor covering in the drawing-room; the stairs were also covered with sailcloth, stencilled with a chequerboard pattern which proved robust and resilient.

Much of Mackintosh's seat furniture was very simply upholstered in horsehair or rush. The sides and back of the tall enclosed 'lug' chair at Mains Street were covered in linen with drawn thread work; while the 1902 white-painted oak chair designed for the Rose Boudoir at Turin had a loose canvas back, stencilled with a rose, and rose silk seat upholstery. The more precious painted chairs might be upholstered in a richer material, such as the purple velvet used to cover the seats of the high-backed chairs in the Room de Luxe at the Willow Tea Rooms. Built-in corner or banquette seating often had stencilled designs applied to the back rests.

Towards the end of his career, Mackintosh supplemented his dwindling income by designing fabrics, sold principally to two firms, Foxton's and Sefton's. Textile design was a new field of endeavour for him; none of his previous designs for fabric had been produced for commercial printing, merely stencilled or embroidered and conceived for a specific application within a particular interior. During the period between 1915 and 1923 he produced over 120 different designs in this new medium, ranging from patterns based on stylized flowers and natural forms to more abstract motifs, vibrant and undulating designs that look forward to Art Deco.

It is not known how many of these designs were put into production; only two of the surviving samples of fabrics produced by Foxton's can be ascribed to Mackintosh with any certainty. From what records remain, Mackintosh appears to have earned a respectable amount from this work and it is reasonable to assume that his continuing association with the two firms must have resulted in many other designs being put into production. Occasionally notes on the original drawings indicate the type of fabric in which a design was to be produced. Since these range from silk and voile to furnishing materials, it is likely that the fabrics found a variety of applications, both in clothing and interior decoration.

A large number of these designs were based on simple stylized flowers and organic forms – roses, tulips, chrysanthemums, dahlias and tobacco flowers. The watercolour studies and paintings Mackintosh also produced during this time, which are among the best of his artistic career, provided an obvious source of inspiration. Around the same period, Mackintosh and his wife collaborated on a

Four of Mackintosh's fabric designs, currently in production. Clockwise, from top left: Rose and Teardrop, Tulip and Lattice (in two colourways), and Rectangles and Green Checks. In Rose and Teardrop, each of the twenty roses in the repeat is different.

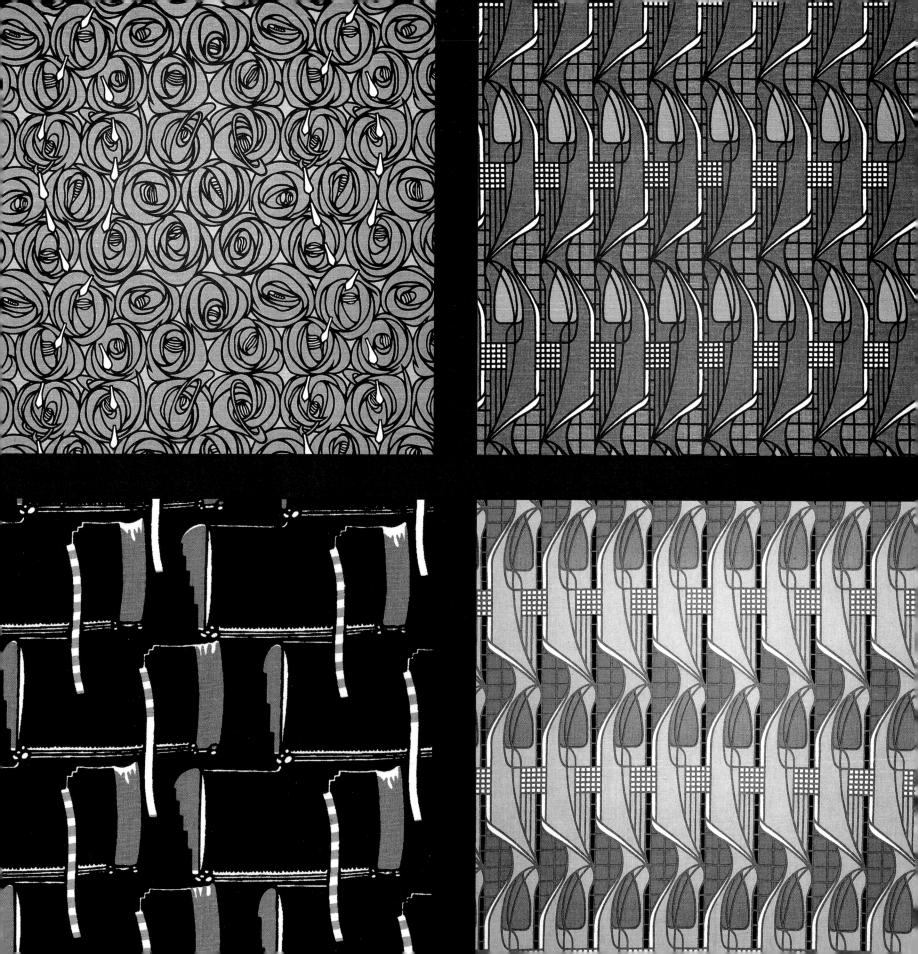

work called *The Voices in the Wood* (exhibited in 1916 at the Arts and Crafts Exhibition Society's Eleventh Exhibition), which displays a number of motifs featured in some of the textile designs. A related pair of paintings, *The Little Hills*, was created for The Dug-Out, the final Glasgow tea-room commission.

The textile designs, particularly the bold abstract patterns of geometric shapes, are another aspect of the new design direction Mackintosh was exploring in the Derngate interiors and furniture. Like the Derngate designs, these textiles show some affinity with contemporary Austrian and German work, some of which was published in Britain before the First World War. The vivid primary colours in rippling or wavelike patterns on dark backgrounds echo the theme of the black entrance hall at Derngate.

The spare, linear quality of Mackintosh's early designs for fabrics is entirely missing in these bright, crowded patterns, alive with movement and rich with colour. Mackintosh appears to have mastered the medium rapidly, adapting his characteristic motifs to the new technique. The undulating form of many of the designs shows an instinctive appreciation of how pattern can complement and express the flowing folds of gathered fabric, while his suggestions for alternative colourways also display a thorough understanding of how to manipulate the dynamic of a print. And, as ever, aspects of his work in this field anticipated what was to come. When the jazz colours and bold geometries of Art Deco exploded on to the decorative scene at the Exposition des Arts Décoratifs in Paris in 1925, Mackintosh had already abandoned design and architecture for good.

■ ■ ■

MACK-INTOSH TODAY

MACKINTOSH'S CONTEMPORARY REPUTATION – SUCH AS IT WAS – RESTED ALMOST ENTIRELY ON HIS work as a furniture and interior designer. During his short career he designed over 400 pieces of furniture, many of which were 'one-offs', created for a specific interior and, often, for a specific location within that interior. The fact that none of these designs was ever produced in any great number has largely been responsible for the astronomical saleroom prices individual pieces fetch today.

One of the criticisms which surfaced from time to time throughout Mackintosh's career concerned practicality. Even his great supporter, Muthesius, voiced an element of doubt when he wondered whether the sublime artistry of the white interiors was really appropriate for everyday living. 'Even a book in an unsuitable binding would disturb the atmosphere simply by lying on the table, indeed even the man or woman of today – especially the man in his unadorned working attire – treads like a stranger in this fairytale world.'

Mackintosh's clients, however, were never dissatisfied by the practical aspects of the homes he created for them. In his architectural work, he was highly attuned to everyday needs, whether of a

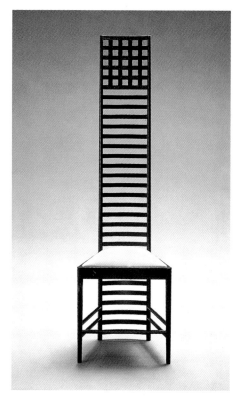

A number of Mackintosh chairs are manufactured today by the Italian firm Cassina, working under licence from the University of Glasgow and adhering closely to the original designs or prototypes. These include the chair with oval back rail designed for the Argyle Street Tea Rooms in 1897, the ladderback chair from the bedroom at The Hill House (1902) and the high-backed chair designed in 1900 for the White Dining Room at Ingram Street Tea Rooms.

household or a school of art, and all his buildings function well at this essential level. Nevertheless, his best work was created for those who shared his own artistic outlook and who would not have found it confining to operate within the terms he set.

It is certainly true that Mackintosh designs do not lend themselves to a piecemeal or eclectic approach, where a variety of pieces from different periods are thrown together in a happy, sympathetic blend. At the same time, a pair of high-backed chairs will not by themselves create a Mackintosh interior, nor is it easy to duplicate the artistry of Mackintosh decoration. The simplicity of his work fell short of minimalism and it is clear that this direction ultimately held no attraction for him. But modern rooms with their minimal detailing and lower ceiling heights probably provide a better starting-point for those interested in recapturing at least some of the unique ambience of the original interiors.

A more damning charge concerns the relatively poor performance of some of Mackintosh's chairs. In the case of the high-backed chair designed for the bedroom at The Hill House, which is particularly frail structurally, the functional weakness reflects the fact that the chair was intended to serve as a

In the bedroom of an Edinburgh flat, designer Alan Day creates his own interpretation of the Mackintosh style (LEFT AND RIGHT), using the familiar motif of the square in glass inserts on wardrobe doors and as applied decoration on the bed cover. Reproductions of Mackintosh's Hill House and Ingram Street chairs anchor the arrangement of the room.

spatial marker within the context of the arrangement of that room, rather than be in regular use for seating. But many of tea-room chairs, which were most definitely designed to be sat on, also proved far from robust in everyday use. The ladder-back chairs designed for the Willow Tea Rooms subsequently often had to be braced along the upper rail, a remedial feature which was retained in the Cassina facsimile of this design. The Windsor chairs Mackintosh created for the Library at the School of Art did not survive well either, and only six of the originals remain. And no one has ever claimed that a Mackintosh chair provides a comfortable perch for any length of time.

The first commercial indication of the rehabilitation of his reputation was seen in 1975, when a Mackintosh chair originally designed for Hous'hill was sold at auction to an American collector for £9,300 ($14,400). In 1973, following an exhibition at the *Triennale* in Milan, four of the original designs were put into production by the Milan-based company Cassina in a form approved by the copyright holders, the University of Glasgow: the high-backed chair with oval back rail from the Argyle Street

The delicacy of the ladderback chair (LEFT) *designed for the bedroom at The Hill House reflects its original function as a spatial marker, a graphic counterpoint to the large pieces of white painted furniture.*

Tea Rooms (1897), the ladder-back Willow Tea Rooms chair (1903), the Hill House bedroom chair (1903) and the semicircular lattice-back order desk chair for the Willow Tea Rooms (1904). This catalogue has since been expanded to include twenty different designs, all of which are conspicuously faithful to the originals.

Today, interest in Mackintosh's work has become so intense that clocks, light fittings, stencils, tiles, jewellery, cutlery and textiles are also in current production. In some cases, designs are reproduced as accurately as possible, and provide a good source for those who wish to acquire a version of a Mackintosh design for their home. Riding the tide of popular interest, other 'Mackintosh-inspired' artefacts and furnishings have also flourished in recent years, particularly after the design copyright expired in 1978. Far too often, such designs more than merit their popular designation, 'Mockintosh'. It is hard to imagine the 'artist architect' would really have approved.

The poetic nature of Mackintosh interiors remains inspirational today. This arrangement (RIGHT) *features a version of the Ingram Street chair, together with a Mackintosh-style fabric design and stencilled decoration.*

The Artist's Cottage at Farr, near Inverness, was built in 1992 from an unexecuted design prepared by Mackintosh in 1900. The owners, Peter and Maxine Tovell, commissioned Robert Hamilton to realize the project, using the four elevational drawings and floor plan of the original scheme. The building, which incorporates a studio, is thought to have been intended as a country home for Mackintosh and his wife. The house comprises a two-storey cube with a single-storey extension to one side.

Mackintosh was working at a time when the domestic interior was in transition from the formal and public showcase of previous centuries to a more private and intimate domain, a place of retreat and refuge. His rooms do not fall neatly within the category of a particular style or period, but represent an original and artistic response to interior space. As such, they cannot readily be recreated via a type of design blueprint, although it is possible to identify certain strands of his approach which have had an impact on contemporary interior design and remain relevant today.

Unpicking the elements of a Mackintosh interior rapidly becomes a circular exercise; the strands are so interwoven that to start in one place inevitably entails finishing in another. If these rooms have anything to teach us, it is to conceive an interior, or house, in its entirety and not to strive for isolated effects. The best of Mackintosh's work displays a sublime poise, where decorative and structural aspects are held in a delicate balance. This, above all, is the essence of the Mackintosh style.

Interior detail at the Artist's Cottage is faithful to the spirit of Mackintosh's original design (RIGHT). *Leaded glass panels with motifs taken from a variety of Mackintosh sources are inset into the windows* (ABOVE).

Elements of the Mackintosh style are present in many of our homes today. In modern houses and apartments, the physical proportions of the rooms, the long low lines, the simple mouldings or architraves, and the general absence of architectural clutter are direct descendants of the style. Open-plan or split-level interiors, with interconnecting spaces screened by latticed panels and open dividers, owe at least some debt to Mackintosh's approach. If we enjoy decorative simplicity, plain screened windows which suffuse a room with sunlight, the graphic contrast of glossy black and soft white, our tastes may have unwittingly been shaped by the ideas he first expressed nearly a century ago. Since that date, of course, there have been many more architects and designers who have had direct and visible impact on the formation of contemporary style. But Mackintosh was among the first to conceive interiors in this way, and the anticipatory nature of his work has kept it fresh and original to this day.

Those enamoured of the Mackintosh style are inevitably drawn to acquire some version of his designs for their own interiors. If his furniture was often very specific in conception, individual pieces have also proved iconographic, even sculptural in their own right. Standing in its own space, within a sympathetic contemporary setting, a Mackintosh chair retains its architectural power and graphic impact. At least some of the pieces reproduced in the Cassina collection can also function on a more practical level. The oval-back chair from the Argyle Street Tea Rooms works as well as a dining-chair today as it did when it was first designed, forming a private enclosure or palisade around the table. The boxy armchair and upholstered settee designed originally for the Argyle Street smoking room anchor the arrangement of a contemporary living space.

It would be impossible, of course, to furnish an entire house with Mackintosh pieces; and it is equally difficult to recapture the unique decorative atmosphere of his original interiors. But that is not the point. The basic principles embodied by these interiors, astonishing and radical for their time, are now integral to the way we organize and conceive our homes. At the least, we can relish the vibrancy of one of his late textile designs hanging at the window; light our living-room with the Rose Lamps first designed for Miss Cranston; stencil bands of Mackintosh motifs in the hallway; or decorate the front door with a pattern of coloured glass squares – and enjoy our simple homage to this great and complex designer.

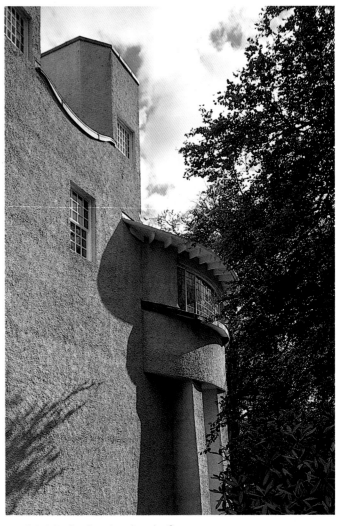

The proposal to construct 'The Art-lover's House' in Glasgow's Bellahouston Park is the most ambitious scheme yet undertaken to reproduce one of Mackintosh's unbuilt designs. Nearing completion, the building will eventually house an international study centre for architecture and the visual arts. Considerable care has been taken to interpret Mackintosh's intentions and translate his drawings.

APPENDICES

PLACES TO VISIT

■

SCOTLAND

As well as the following places to visit, there are various buildings in and around Glasgow which were designed partially or completely by Mackintosh. Access may not be possible, but exteriors can always be viewed. These include the Glasgow Herald Building, the Martyr's Public School, Ruchill Church Hall, the Daily Record Building and the Ladies' Art Club.

The Glasgow School of Art
167 Renfrew Street, Glasgow G3 5RQ
(tel 0141–332 9797)
Mackintosh's masterpiece, still functioning as a school of art. Guided tours available; shop selling books, guides, posters and catalogues, as well as selected products made to Mackintosh designs. The Mackintosh Room and Furniture Gallery house an important collection, including much of the furniture and fittings from Windyhill, donated by the Davidson family.

Queen's Cross Church
870 Garscube Road, Glasgow G20 7EL
(tel 0141–946 6600)
Headquarters of the Charles Rennie Mackintosh Society. Tours and special 'Mackintosh' weekends organized in conjunction with Glasgow Tourist Board. Posters, books, catalogues and guides available from the shop, including a range of jewellery inspired by Mackintosh designs. The Society publishes a quarterly newsletter.

Willow Tea Rooms
217 Sauchiehall Street, Glasgow G2 3EX
(tel 0141–332 0521)
The Room de Luxe has been partially restored and is open for teas. The remainder of the building is occupied by a jeweller's and gift shop.

Scotland Street School
Scotland Street, Glasgow G5 8QB (tel 0141–429 1202)
Recently restored, the school now functions as a Museum of Education.

Hunterian Art Gallery (The Mackintosh House)
University of Glasgow, Hillhead Street, Glasgow G12 8QQ (tel 0141–330 5431)
Reconstructed Mackintosh interiors, incorporating furniture and fittings from 78 Southpark Avenue, and the reconstructed Derngate guest bedroom.

The Hill House
Upper Colquhoun Street, Helensburgh G84 9AJ, Dunbartonshire (tel 01436–73900)
Mackintosh's finest domestic building, recently restored and administered by the National Trust for Scotland.

Art Gallery and Museum
Kelvingrove, Glasgow G3 8AG (tel 0141–357 3929)
Paintings, artefacts and furniture by practitioners of the Glasgow Style on display.

The Art Lover's House
Bellahouston Park, Dumbreck Road
Glasgow, As yet incomplete reconstruction of Mackintosh's 1901 design.

UNITED STATES

Metropolitan Museum of Art
1000 Fifth Avenue, New York, NY 10028-0198,
(tell 212 879-5500)
Collection of 20th century designs and furniture, including pieces by Mackintosh.

Virginia Museum of Fine Arts
2800 Grove Avenue, Richmond, Virginia 23221-2466,
(tel 804 367-0844)
Includes beautiful pieces of furniture and cutlery by Mackintosh

ENGLAND

The Victoria and Albert Museum, London
The most important collection of 19th and 20th century British furniture in the world; some Mackintosh textile designs.

FRANCE

Musée d'Orsay, Paris
Fine collection of 19th and 20th century art and furniture, including pieces by Webb, Voysey, Hoffmann, Moser and Mackintosh.

AUSTRIA

Österreichisches Museum für angewandte Kunst, Vienna
Pieces by Voysey, Baillie Scott and Mackintosh and other British designers exhibiting in Europe at the turn of the century.

NORWAY

Nordenfjeldske Kunstindistri Museum, Trondheim
Arts and Crafts and Art Noveau collection, including works by Walton and Mackintosh.

SOURCES OF MACKINTOSH DESIGNS

■

EUROPE

Cassina S.p.A.
PO Box 134, 20036 Meda, Milan, Italy
(tel 00(39) 362 372)
Produce many pieces of furniture to original Mackintosh designs, licensed by the copyright holders. Pieces include the Rose Lamp from Hous'hill, tables, and chairs such as The Hill House bedroom chair, lattice back order desk chair from the Willow Tea Rooms and the Argyle Street chair.

SCP Limited
135–9 Curtain Road
London EC2A 3BX (tel 0171–739 1869)
Stockists of authentic reproduction classic designs from the 20th century, including Mackintosh and Hoffmann furniture.

FREUD Limited
198 Shaftesbury Avenue
London WC2H 8JL (tel 0171–831 1071)
Stockists of Cassina reproductions of Mackintosh furniture.

In House
24–26 Wilson Street
Glasgow G1 1SS (tel 0141–552 5902)
Stockists of Cassina collection, including Rose Lamp.

Alexander Beauchamp
Yulcan House, Stratton Road
Gloucester GL1 4HL (tel 01452–384 959)
Wallpaper inspired by Mackintosh designs.

Sabattini Argenterie
Bregnano, Como, Italy
Vases, cutlery, candlesticks, trays, carafes manufactured to Mackintosh designs under sub-licence from Cassina.

IS
Bologna, Italy
Mackintosh Derngate clock, manufactured to Mackintosh design under sub-licence from Cassina.

Bute Fabrics
Isle of Bute, Scotland
Fabrics produced to original Mackintosh designs.

Beaten Path Studio
Cotton Street, Castle Douglas DG7 1AR
Selection of fabrics, in a variety of colourways, produced to original Mackintosh designs. Fabrics are printed by hand on 100% cotton; designs include 'Tulip and Lattice', 'Rose and Teardrop', 'Rectangles and Green Checks', 'Stylised Flowers' and 'Chequerwork'.

Tadema 1900, Decorative Arts
10 Charlton Place
London N1 8AJ (tel 0171–359 0396)
Original Art Nouveau jewellery, including work by Jessie King and others of the Glasgow School, as available.

Charles Rennie Mackintosh Society
Queen's Cross Church
870 Garscube Road
Glasgow G20 7EU (tel 0141–946 6600)
Jewellery inspired by Mackintosh designs, by Ola Gorie.

SOURCES OF MACKINTOSH DESIGNS

UNITED STATES

Arkitektura In-Situ
474 North Woodward, Birmingham, MI 48009
(tel: 313-646-0097; fax: 313-646-0823)

Axis 20
200 Peachtree Hills Avenue NE, Atlanta, GA 30305
(tel: 404-261-4022; fax: 404-237-5351)

Bentwood, The
8 Eastgate, Chapel Hill, NC 27514
(tel: 919-967-6789; fax: 919-968-1441)

Cassina Showroom
155 East 56th Streeet, New York, NY 1,0022
(tel: 212-245-2121; fax: 212-245-1340)

Contract Furniture Consultants Inc.
178-B South Monaco Parkway, Denver, CO 80224
(tel: 303-321-4892; fax: 303-446-0146)

Current
1201 Western Avenue, Seattle, WA 98101
(tel: 206-622-2433; fax: 206-622-8605)

Diva
8801 Beverly Blvd, Los Angeles, CA 90048
(tel: 310-278-3191; fax: 310-274-7189)

Ferguson/Rice
20 Greenway Plaza, Suite 210, Houston, TX 77046
(tel: 713-965-9085; fax: 713-965-9641)

Full Upright Position
1101 N.W. Gleason, Portland, OR 97209
(tel: 503-228-6213; fax: 503-228-6213)

Holly Hunt Ltd
275 Market Street, Minneapolis, MN 55405
(tel: 612-332-1900; fax: 612-332-6179)

Howard Fishman Associates
11332 Old Ranch Circle, Chatsworth, CA 91311
(tel: 818-718-9402; fax: 818-773-8574)

J.L. Gelbart
15 Millrock Road, Hamden, CT 06517
(tel: 203-776-1010; fax: 203-776-2100)

Light Spot
1043 East 900 South, Salt Lake City, UT 84105
(tel: 801-322-5500; fax: 801-322-1431)

Light Spot
1516 Wazee Street, Denver, CO 80202
(tel: 303-446-2284; fax: 303-446-0416)

Limn
290 Townsend Street, San Francisco, CA 94107
(tel; 415-543-5466; fax: 415-543-5971)

Lloyd Scott
1400 Turtle Creek, Suite 203, Dallas, TX 75207
(tel: 214-748-9838; fax: 214-748-5006)

Luminaire
301 West Superior Street, Chicago, IL 60610
(tel: 312-664-9582; fax: 312-664-5045)

Luminaire
7300 Southwest 45 Street, Miami, FL 33155
(tel: 305-264-6308; fax: 305-264-2181)

Montage
One Design Center Place, Suite 233, Boston, MA 02210
(tel: 617-451-1181; fax: 617-451-6762)

Mossa Center
1214 Washington Avenue, Saint Louis, MO 63103
(tel: 314-241-5199; fax: 314-241-0711)

MPLA Associates
444 S. Cedros, Studio 170, Solana Beach, CA 92075
(tel: 619-481-9209; fax: 619-481-6667)

O.L.C.
152-154 N. Third Street, Philadelphia, PA 19106
(tel: 215-923-6085; fax: 215-351-1215)

Russin Associates
4877 Shac:kelford Court, Columbus, OH 43220
(tel: 614-457-4694; fax: 614-457-4075)

Sylvia Sturm
1718 M street N.W. #237, Washington D.C. 20036
(tel: 202-387-8509; fax: 202-387-8536)

ACKNOWLEDGEMENTS

■ ■ ■

The publisher thanks the photographers and organizations for their kind permission to reproduce the following photographs in this book:

2 The Interior World/Fritz von der Schulenburg; **6** Glasgow School of Art; **9** Hunterian Art Gallery/University of Glasgow Collection (photo Media Services Photographic Unit); **12** The Edinburgh Photographic Library/ David Morrison; **15** Glasgow School of Art; **16** Glasgow Room, Mitchell Library/J Irvine; **18** The Annan Collection, Glasgow; **19-21** Glasgow School of Art; **22** The Annan Collection, Glasgow; **25** Hunterian Art Gallery/University of Glasgow (photo Media Services Photographic Unit); **26** Glasgow School of Art; **27** Scotland Street School/Museum of Education; **28** Glasgow School of Art; **29** Philippe Garner; **31** The Annan Collection, Glasgow; **32** Glasgow School of Art; **33** Copyright British Museum; **34** Glasgow School of Art; **36** Hunterian Art Gallery; **39** Edifice/Philippa Lewis; **40** Country Life Picture Library; **41** Ianthe Ruthven; **42** ET Archive/Tate Gallery; **43** ET Archive; **44** Courtesy of the Board of Trustees of the Victoria and Albert Museum; **45** ET Archive/Oriental Art Museum, Genoa; **46** ET Archive; **47** Philippe Garner; **49** Glasgow Museums: Art Gallery & Museums/Kelvingrove; **50** Philippe Garner; **51** Glasgow Museums; **52** ET Archive; **55** Bastian & Evrard; **56** The Interior World/Fritz von der Schulenburg; **56** Anzenberger/Toni Anzenberger; **57** Bastian & Evrard; **58-60** Sotheby's London; **62** The Edinburgh Photographic Library/David Morrison; **64** Glasgow School of Art; **65-66** The Edinburgh Photographic Library/David Morrison; **69** Martin Charles; **71** Glasgow School of Art; **73** Arcaid/David Churchill; **73** Martin Charles; **74** left Martin Charles; **74** right Glasgow School of Art; **75** Edifice/Philippa Lewis; **76** Arcaid; **78** above Arcaid; **79** Edinburgh Photographic Library/Ralph Burnett; **80** Edinburgh Photographic Library/David Morrison; **83** Glasgow School of Art; **85** The Annan Collection, Glasgow; **87** Arcaid/Richard Bryant; **89** The Interior World/Fritz von der Schulenburg; **95** The Edinburgh Photographic Library/Ralph Burnett; **96** The Interior World/Fritz von der Schulenburg; **99** Arcaid/Ken Kirkwood; **100-101** Edinburgh Photographic Library/Ralph Burnett; **102-104** Arcaid/Ken Kirkwood; **105** Ianthe Ruthven; **106** left The Annan Collection, Glasgow; **106** right Glasgow School of Art; **109** Angelo Hornak; **110** Glasgow School of Art; **111** Edinburgh Photographic Library/Ralph Burnett; **112** Edinburgh Photographic Library; **113-115** Hunterian Art Gallery/University of Glasgow Collection (Photo Media Services Photographic Unit); **117** Ianthe Ruthven; **118** Hunterian Art Gallery/University of Glasgow Collection (Photo Media Services Photographic Unit); **120-123** The Interior World/Fritz von der Schulenburg; **124** Ianthe Ruthven; **127** Arcaid; **129** The Interior World/Fritz von der Schulenburg; **130** Glasgow School of Art; **131** Arcaid/Ken Kirkwood; **132-135** Ianthe Ruthven; **136** The Interior World/Fritz von der Schulenburg; **137** Sabattini Argenteria SpA; **138** left Sotheby's London; **138** right Sotheby's London; **141-143** Ianthe Ruthven; **145** Beaten Path Studio; **147** Cassina SpA; **148** Arcaid/Ken Kirkwood (designer Alan Day); **149** The Imrie-Tait Partnership/ *Country Life* Picture Library; **150** Ianthe Ruthven; **151** Elizabeth Whiting & Assocaiates; **152** The Imrie-Tait Partnership/*Country Life* Picture Library; **153** left The Imrie-Tait Partnership/*Country Life* Picture Library; **153** right Simon Jauncy; **154-155** The Glasgow Picture Library/ Eric Thorburn.

SELECTED BIBLIOGRAPHY

■

ALISON, Filippo   *Charles Rennie Mackintosh as a designer of chairs* Academy Editions, London, 1978

BILLCLIFFE, Roger   *Charles Rennie Mackintosh, The Complete Furniture, Furniture Drawings and Interior Designs*   Lutterworth Press, London, 1979 *Mackintosh Furniture*   Cameron and Hollis, 1984   *Charles Rennie Mackintosh, Textile Designs* Pomegranate Artbooks, California, 1993

BRETT, David   *Charles Rennie Mackintosh, The Poetics of Workmanship* Reaktion Books, London, 1992

BUCHANAN, William, ed.   *Mackintosh's Masterwork, The Glasgow School of Art*   Richard Drew Publishing, Glasgow, 1989

COOPER, Jackie, ed.   *Mackintosh Architecture, The Complete Buildings and Selected Projects*   Academy Editions, London, 1978

HACKNEY, Fiona and Isla   *Charles Rennie Mackintosh*   The Apple Press, London, 1989

HOWARTH, Thomas   *Charles Rennie Mackintosh and the Modern Movement*   Routledge and Kegan Paul, London, second edition 1977

JONES, Anthony   *Charles Rennie Mackintosh*   Studio Editions, London, 1990

KINCHIN, Perilla   *Tea and Taste, The Glasgow Tea Rooms 1875–1975* White Cockade Publishing, 1991

LARNER, Gerald and Celia   *The Glasgow Style*   Paul Harris Publishing, Edinburgh, 1979

MACAULAY, James   *Glasgow School of Art*   Phaidon Press, London, 1993

MACLEOD, Robert   *Charles Rennie Mackintosh*   Country Life Books, London, 1968

MOFFAT, Alistair   *Remembering Charles Rennie Mackintosh, an illustrated biography*   Colin Baxter Photography Ltd, Lanark, 1989

NEAT, Timothy   *Part Seen, Part Imagined, Meaning and Symbolism in the Work of Charles Rennie Mackintosh and Margaret Macdonald*   Canongate Press, Edinburgh, 1994

ROBERTSON, Pamela, ed.   *Charles Rennie Mackintosh: The Architectural Papers*   White Cockade Publishing, 1990

YOUNG, Andrew McLaren   *Charles Rennie Mackintosh, Architecture, Design and Painting*   Exhibition catalogue, Edinburgh Festival Society, 1968

INDEX

Page numbers in italics refer to illustrations